Disaggregating Data in Schools

LEVERAGING THE INFORMATION YOU HAVE

By
Paige Leavitt
Randy McDaniel
Emma Skogstad

APQC.
PUBLICATIONS

American Productivity & Quality Center
123 North Post Oak Lane, Third floor
Houston, TX 77024

Edited by Kristin Arnold of EdVance, with Nadia Uddin
Designed by Fred Bobovnyk Jr
Cover Designed by Connie Choate

Manufactured in the United States of America

ISBN 1-932546-07-3

American Productivity & Quality Center
Web site address: www.apqc.org/pubs

Table of Contents

Preface

At the heart of the debate of the merit of the No Child Left Behind (NCLB) act is this nation's ongoing dilemma concerning standards. Despite compelling questions raised about the validity and relevance of certain standardized tests, the United States has largely proceeded with such testing, as well as the requisite expectations for results from the campus to the national level, under the simple premise that we must start somewhere.

The motivation for standardized tests at the K-12 level is compelling: to ensure that students keep up with the curriculum so that teachers can focus on progressively more challenging lesson plans, instead of continually needing to catch students up. With course curricula varying in each classroom, the U.S. education system has had significantly varied expectations of various students. As shared in *The State Education Standard*[1],

> In survey after survey, these young people are telling us that
> they are not being challenged in school. The situation is worse
> in high-poverty and high-minority schools. ...Clear and
> public standards for what students should learn at
> benchmark grade levels are a critical part of solving this
> problem. They are a guide—for teachers, administrators,
> parents, and students themselves—to what knowledge and
> skills are critical for students to master. ...There is now
> ample evidence that almost all children can achieve at high
> levels if they are taught at high levels.

Just as businesses must measure their output, educators are now tasked with measuring their success on a standardized basis. Across any industry, including education, a good plan involves setting goals, identifying target audiences and timelines, and assigning responsibility. The NCLB act sets out the framework for such a plan, with regard to student performance, recognition of diversity, system

---

[1] "State Policy Levers: Closing the Achievement Gap." *The State Education Standard,* Winter 2002.

stability, statutory compliance, appropriate consequences, local program flexibility, local responsibility, and the public's right to know.

This framework means that educators are tasked with more than just reporting results. The mandate is now clearer than ever for educators, from teachers to district administrators, to act on those results to improve each student's performance. A single composite score for a school will likely be of little use to educators. Instead, they will need to leverage any relevant and valid existing data and break down the data into individual elements for greater meaning that can be applied to the campus and the classroom.

To proceed, all educators will need an understanding of why it is important to disaggregate data, how leveraging data can lead to more informed decision making, and how to interpret results. This book will detail how to read terminology and test results correctly and how to make the most of the data you already have in hand, both from the NCLB act and other existing sources, to improve student performance, instead of simply assuming where there are problems.

This book proceeds on the premise that all children can learn and that all educators play a part in ensuring that no child is left behind. In short, the impetus for disaggregating data is fairness and the absolute need to continually improve this nation's educational system. Both district and campus level staff and teachers can benefit from using the terms and ideas presented in this book to initiate a common dialogue for continuous improvement.

Chapter 1

Data Disaggregation: What Is It and Why Is It Necessary?

Signed by President Bush with overwhelming bipartisan support in January 2002, the No Child Left Behind (NCLB) act aims to improve the achievement of the nation's schools and children by giving individual schools and districts greater control and flexibility and by holding schools accountable for their results. The ultimate goal is to provide all children with access to high-quality education and to prevent children from being denied their basic right to quality instruction.

An important cornerstone of the NCLB act is data disaggregation. Through the act, data is used to identify groups of students who may not be fully benefiting from a state's educational program and to focus resources and actions to assist those groups of students to meet standards. By focusing on the progress of different types of students, data disaggregation ensures all students are well-treated within the system. (However, a cautionary argument is that if schools are challenged on improving performance, then certain groups will be targeted at the expense of others.)

> Data disaggregation is the act of acquiring relevant information and then disseminating it to interested parties for further data analysis.

Many lawmakers and other supporters of the NCLB act hope that by targeting academic achievement early in the adolescent years, they will increase the learning potential of every child. For example, research shows that most reading problems faced by adolescents and adults could have been prevented through good instruction in their early childhood years[2]. The NCLB act targets resources for early childhood education so that all children get the right start.

NCLB Act Guidelines

The guiding ideas behind the NCLB act embody four key principles: stronger accountability for results; greater flexibility for states, school districts, and schools in the use of federal funds; more choices for parents of children from disadvantaged backgrounds; and an emphasis on teaching methods that have been demonstrated to work[3].

The NCLB act is resulting in fundamental reforms in classrooms throughout America. It is redefining the federal role in K-12 education to help improve the academic achievement of all American students. By reauthorizing the Elementary and Secondary Education Act (ESEA) of 1965, the NCLB act incorporates the strategies and principles enforced by President Bush.

Accountability

Through increased accountability, the NCLB act takes major steps in closing the significant achievement gap that exists between disadvantaged and minority students and their more affluent and/or Caucasian peers[4].

Although every state has had some accountability systems in place based on student achievement, many of these systems excluded schools from accountability or set lower criteria. The requirement that states create annual assessments to measure children's reading and math ability in grades 3 through 8 and once in high school allows everyone—parents, educators, administrators, and politicians—to track the performance of every school in the nation. Data is now being disaggregated for most student groups, sometimes not including children of migrant workers, and tracked over time to ensure that no child is left behind.

---

[2] U.S. Department of Education, No Child Left Behind Web site, www.ed.gov, retrieved June 2003.

[3] U.S. Department of Education, *No Child Left Behind: A Desktop Reference*, 2002.

[4] U.S. Department of Education, Office of Elementary and Secondary Education, *On the Horizon: State Accountability Systems*, October 2002.

This means that assessment results and state progress objectives must be broken down by poverty, race, ethnicity, disability, and limited English proficiency[5]. The data disaggregation demonstrates not only students' overall achievement, but also progress in closing the achievement gap between disadvantaged students and other groups of students.

States are responsible for having strong academic standards for what every child should know in reading, math, and science for elementary, middle, and high schools. Since the 2002 to 2003 school year, schools must administer tests in each of three grade spans: grades 3 through 5, grades 6 through 9, and grades 10 through 12 in all schools. Beginning in the 2005 to 2006 school year, tests must be administered every year in grades 3 through 8 and once in high school. Beginning in the 2007 to 2008 school year, science achievement must also be tested[6].

The federal government will provide some assistance to help states design and administer these tests. The president and Congress have provided some resources to help pay for testing, beginning with $387 million in 2002 to help states develop and administer reading and math tests. The president's 2003 budget requested another $387 million[7]. For the 2004 fiscal year, $500 million is set aside for school-improvement efforts nationally.

[5] U.S. Department of Education, *The No Child Left Behind Act of 2001*, Executive Summary.

[6] U.S. Dept of Education Web site, *Raw Data: Data Disaggregation*, www.ed.gov, retrieved July 2003.

[7] U.S. Dept of Education Web site, *Raw Data: Data Disaggregation*, www.ed.gov, retrieved July 2003.

Annual Report Cards

The National Assessment of Educational Progress is an independent benchmark and the only nationally representative and continuing assessment of what American students know and can do in various subject areas, according to the Department of Education. Since 1969, the National Center for Education Statistics has conducted NAEP assessments in reading, mathematics, science, writing, U.S. history, geography, civics, and the arts.

Under the NCLB act, as a condition of receiving federal funding, states are required to participate in the NAEP math and reading assessments twice a year for grades 4 and 8. Resulting data will significantly increase information available to compare the performance of students among states. NAEP data will also highlight the rigor of standards and tests for individual states to reveal large discrepancies (this suggests a need for the state to take a close look at its standards and assessments and consider making improvements).

Annual school report cards now provide comparative information on the quality of schools. The NCLB act requires that these report cards be easy to read and provide thorough information about which schools are succeeding and why. They show not only students' progress in meeting standards, but also the progress disaggregated groups are making in closing the achievement gaps. Included in the report cards is achievement data broken down by race, ethnicity, gender, English-language proficiency, disability status, and low-income status, as well as important information about the professional qualifications of teachers, school attendance, grade retention and promotion, and improvement in ability to read at grade level. These report cards must be available to students' parents promptly and by no later than the beginning of the school year.

In addition to student report cards, schools must also create campus report cards that provide overall results for student learning. These report cards must be disseminated widely through public means. They can be posted online or distributed to the media or through public agencies.

Adequate yearly progress (AYP) is an individual state's measure of yearly progress toward achieving state academic standards. It sets the minimum level of improvement that school districts and schools must achieve each year. States start by defining adequate yearly progress, which is the measurements of academic improvement a school must achieve to ensure that, at the end of 12 years, every student has a mastery of the basics. Each state chooses where to set the initial academic achievement bar based on the lowest-achieving demographic group or on the lowest-achieving schools in the state, whichever is higher. Once the initial bar is established, the state is required to "raise the bar" gradually to reach 100 percent proficiency at the end of 12 years by 2014. The initial bar must be raised after two years, and subsequent thresholds must be raised at least once every three years.

What happens when districts and schools do not make sufficient yearly progress toward state proficiency goals for their students? First they are targeted for assistance, and then they are subject to corrective action and ultimately restructuring. Schools that meet or exceed objectives will be eligible for academic achievement awards. Furthermore, local school districts must notify parents if their child's school has been identified as "needs improvement," "corrective action," or "restructuring." For each case, districts must let parents know the options available to them. Schools will be responsible for improving the academic performance of all students, and there will be consequences for districts and schools that fail to make progress.

To track the results of statewide assessments, a small sample of students in each state will be randomly selected to participate in the fourth- and eight-grade National Assessment of Educational Progress in reading and math every other year to ensure that states have similarly difficult requirements. Obvious outliers (e.g., one state reports 1,500 schools in need of improvement, and another states reports zero schools in need of improvement) are called out by the NAEP to the scrutiny of the media and watchdog groups. In addition, all states must submit plans to the U.S. Department of Education's secretary of education that include evidence they have content and achievement standards and aligned assessments, school report card procedures, and statewide systems for holding schools and districts accountable for the achievement of their students. Those states that do not make an effort to align assessments could potentially receive reduced federal funding.

Within twelve years, all students must perform at a proficient level under their state standards. However, states will set their own standards for each grade, so each state will say how well children should be reading at the end of third grade, for example. Interested parents, families, and taxpayers can look to their state for detailed information about its academic standards.

Flexibility and Local Control

In exchange for accountability for results, states and school districts will have what the federal government describes as unprecedented flexibility in how they can use federal education funds. The intent is to put greater decision-making powers at the local and state levels where educators are most in touch with students' needs.

Since 1966, the federal government has spent $321 billion (in today's dollars) to help educate disadvantaged children[8]. Federal discretionary spending on education has more than doubled since 1996 (Figure 1).

Despite increased spending, fewer than one-third of American fourth graders read proficiently, reading performance has not improved in more than 15 years, and fewer than 20 percent of the nation's 12th graders score proficiently in math. Among the industrialized nations of the world, U.S. 12th graders rank near the bottom in science and math.

To cut down on federal red tape, the NCLB act reduces the overall number of programs from the Elementary and Secondary Education Act (ESEA) and offers most local school districts in America the freedom to transfer up to 50 percent of the federal dollars they receive among several education programs without

---

[8] U.S. Dept of Education Web site, *Raw Data: Data Disaggregation*, www.ed.gov, retrieved July 2003.

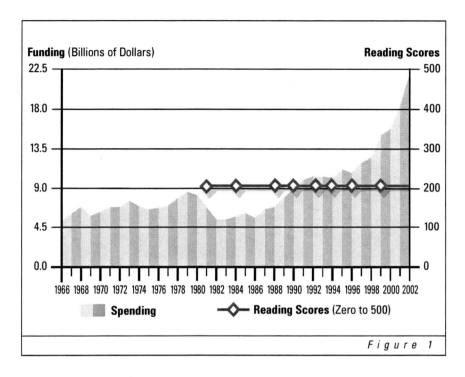

Figure 1

separate approval[9]. The NCLB act makes it possible for most districts to transfer up to 50 percent of the federal formula grant funds they receive under the Improving Teacher Quality State Grants, Educational Technology, Innovative Programs, and Safe and Drug-Free Schools programs to any one of these programs without separate approval. Schools can also use funds to address particular needs, such as hiring new teachers or developing bilingual education programs or professional development strategies. Some states are concerned about the cost of adhering to NCLB act mandates, but some research organizations are finding the mandates fiscally feasible. For instance, the Education Leaders Council commissioned the research firm Accountability Works to look at real costs associated with the new testing requirements. Accountability Works found the average state will spend between $6.1 and $7.6 million adhering to the act and will receive $7.1 million in federal funds for

---

[9] U.S. Department of Education, *Fact Sheet on No Child Left Behind*, www.ed.gov, retrieved July 2003.

this purpose. Because states will have more control over the direction of their federal money, local communities will have more say about which programs they think will most help their students.

In the NCLB mandates, states have several choices about how to adhere to the legislation. For instance, states can identify schools for improvement, corrective action, and restructuring based on a school's not making adequate yearly progress in the same subject for two or more years. Most states, with the current exception of Louisiana, identify schools for improvement only after the school has missed adequate yearly progress in the same subject for consecutive years. States also have flexibility in naming and defining their achievement levels (e.g., basic, proficient, and advanced). Student stakes (i.e., meeting a specific proficiency level), which some states mandate for a student to proceed to the next grade, are not an NCLB mandate.

State flexibility also extends to the setting of minimum group sizes for AYP determinations, reporting, and participation rates. States must consider a number of factors when making this decision, such as student privacy, the average size of schools, the number of tested grades, and the extent of diversity among students. States can also set a different AYP group size for special education students. In addition, they can determine what constitutes a major racial or ethnic subgroup. They can determine grade spans for AYP decisions and decide how many years of data will be used to make an AYP determination—one, two, or an average of three. States can select their other academic indicators and set AYP criteria for these indicators. At the elementary and middle school levels, these indicators vary widely among the states (e.g., attendance rates, retention rate, and achievement on social studies assessments). At the high school level, the NCLB act requires that, at a minimum, states use the graduation rate as an academic indicator. States can then choose another academic indicator for the high school level.

Enhanced Parental Choice

Parents of children in low-performing schools are given a new range of options under the NCLB act, including the choice to change schools. For example, parents with children in schools that fail to meet state standards for at least two consecutive years may transfer their children to a better-performing public school, including a public charter school, within their district. If they do so, then the district must provide transportation, using Title I funds if necessary. Students from low-income families in schools that fail to meet state standards for at least three years are eligible to receive supplemental educational services, including tutoring, after-school services, and summer school.

If a child attends a persistently dangerous school or is a victim of a violent crime while in school, then he or she has the choice to attend a safe school in that district. These options are closely linked to the accountability provisions that give parents information on which schools in their communities are succeeding and which are not. Hence, the choice and supplemental educational services requirements of the law not only help to enhance student achievement, but also provide an incentive for low-performing schools to improve.

If a school fails to make adequate yearly progress for four consecutive years, then the district must implement certain corrective actions to improve the school, such as replacing some staff or fully implementing a new curriculum, as well as continuing to offer public school choice and pay for supplemental services. If a school fails to make adequate yearly progress for five consecutive years, then it will be identified for restructuring. First, it will have to develop a plan and make the necessary arrangements to implement significant alternative governance actions, state takeover, the hiring of a private management contractor, converting to a charter school, or significant staff restructuring. During the restructuring process, parents and children will get public school choice and supplemental services so the children will not be trapped in failing schools and risk being left behind academically.

Focus on What Works

The NCLB act puts a special emphasis on determining what educational programs and practices have been clearly demonstrated as effective through rigorous scientific research. Federal funding is targeted to support programs and teaching methods that have been proven to improve student learning and achievement.

A good example is reading programs. Federal dollars are tied to programs that use scientifically proven ways of teaching children to read. In 2002 $900 million was distributed to states for the White House administration's *Reading First* plan[10]. This program was intended to develop language and reading skills for preschool children, especially those from low-income families. Funds are also available to help teachers strengthen old skills and gain new ones in effective reading instructional techniques. Schools and teachers got a boost from more than $4 billion in 2002, which allows schools to promote teacher quality through training and recruitment.

Also important are funds directed to after-school and other programs that have been scientifically demonstrated to prevent drug use and violence among youths.

Standards to Improve Education

The implementation of school standards has been a topic of some controversy, but many educators now support higher academic standards because they believe standards are the roadmap to reform. Standards provide guideposts for academic achievement, and test results let students and parents know where students are going.

Through standards, schools can have direction toward common academic goals and can unite the community for reform and achievement. Standards can set a high academic bar for the selection of textbooks, lesson plans, and teacher preparation. Accountability systems gather specific, objective data through tests aligned with standards. This information is used to identify strengths and weaknesses in the system. It helps schools focus resources on the best way to promote learning and allows parents to track their child's progress.

Until teachers and parents identify what a student knows and can do, they cannot help him or her improve. As described earlier, under the NCLB act, every state must set clear and high standards

---

[10] U.S. Dept of Education Web site, *Raw Data: Data Disaggregation*, www.ed.gov, retrieved July 2003.

for what students in each grade should know and be able to do in the core academic subjects of reading, math, and science. States then measure each student's progress toward those standards with tests aligned with the higher standards.

The more parents and taxpayers know about the academic achievement of their children and the overall condition of schools, including safety and teacher quality, the more likely they will choose to be involved in the schools and the public school system. Equipped with information about academic results, parents and community members can make better choices and decisions.

General Guidelines for Disaggregation of Student Data

The purpose of disaggregating student data is to ensure equity for all students in opportunity and achievement. To achieve this purpose, statewide data pertinent to the federal Title I Program has been disaggregated in reports to the federal Department of Education. The rationale is that this disaggregation of data can be a tool to address the question: "Are all students meeting challenging standards?" It should be used to identify groups of students who may not be fully benefiting from a state's educational program and to focus resources and actions to assist those groups of students to meet standards.

Students' rights to privacy and the confidentiality of information, such as test scores, often become a concern during data disaggregation. Disaggregated data may be used only when it does not violate these rights. Schools must adhere to the Family Educational Rights & Privacy (FERPA) act, which protects the privacy of education records, establishes the right of students to inspect and review their education records, and provides guidelines for the correction of inaccurate and misleading data through informal and formal hearings.

Sample Guidelines for Disaggregation and Reporting of Student Test Data[11]

The U.S. Department of Education defines *data disaggregation* as "separating a whole into its parts. In education, this term means that test results are sorted into groups of students who are economically disadvantaged, from racial and ethnic minority groups, have disabilities, or have limited English fluency. This practice allows parents and teachers to see more than just the average score for their child's school. Instead, parents and teachers can see how each student group is performing."

For the sake of privacy and accuracy, it is important to follow guidelines for data disaggregation. The following guidelines, which serve as an example, were created for Hawaii. They apply to disaggregated data that is either intended to be made public or might be made public. If there is any question concerning the public availability of the data, then the data is to be treated as if it will be made public.

1. When the purpose of disaggregation is to report subgroup distributions of data (e.g., above average, average, and below average test scores) the subgroup size must be at least 10.

2. When the purpose of disaggregation is to estimate subpopulation parameters (e.g., means or standard deviations) or to conduct statistical parametric tests (e.g., t-test or ANOVA— the analysis of variance among groups), the subgroups or subgroups for which such calculations are made must be at least 30 in size.

These guidelines do not apply in situations where there is no issue relating to privacy or the revelation of confidential information. For example, there is no bar to a simple descriptive tabulation of a school's population by ethnicity, sex, and other relevant characteristics as long as the tabulation does not potentially

---

[11] http://doe.k12.hi.us/technology/dataqualitydisaggregation.htm, retrieved February 2003.

reveal protected information, such as special education status. The categories of information that should be assumed to raise issues of confidentiality are:

- special education status,
- limited English proficiency status,
- eligibility for free or reduced cost lunch, and
- Section 504 eligibility (which is based on recognition of a disability).

If a breakdown of student data is provided to school professional personnel under assurance of confidentiality, then the above guidelines may also be waived. In such cases, however, it is imperative that all personnel receiving such data must be fully informed of its confidential nature and properly instructed on the protection of confidential data.

The National Perspective

Testing students is nothing new. Good teachers have always tried to measure how well their students are learning and have used tests to recognize student achievement and uncover learning problems. Many believe that without a measurement for student achievement, the only criteria governing student grades and promotion would be behavior in class and attendance.

Testing has recently emerged as an issue because taxpayers are asking more and tougher questions about the performance of their schools and students and are seeking more and better information about school and student performance. The results of teacher-designed exams and a wide assortment of "off the shelf" tests are helpful, but they provide little insight on school performance and academic program impact. The NCLB act is based on the premise that a strong accountability system composed of annual testing keyed to rigorous academic standards and a challenging curriculum taught in the school provides the sort of information needed to determine what works, what does not, how well students are achieving, and what to do to help those who are not achieving. As the use of standardized tests increases and as parents have access to school and student performance information, low-performing schools will have increased pressure to improve.

A number of research efforts regularly examine how state assessments align with scores on NAEP tests, the SAT, the ACT, and advanced placement tests, but there is no consensus among educators across the nation about how improvements on state assessments translate into success in other measurable ways. Skeptics question the fairness and relevance of identifying the SAT, the ACT, advanced placement tests, and the national math and reading exams as determinates of academic performance, even if they are the only nationally administered tests with which to measure one state against another. However, the bottom line of the NCLB mandates is that progress must begin somewhere to instill accountability and ensure every student improves as a result of the system.

> "Accountability is an exercise in hope. When we raise academic standards, children raise their academic sights. When children are regularly tested, teachers know where and how to improve. When scores are known to parents, parents are empowered to push for change. When accountability for our schools is real, the results for our children are real."
>
> —President George W. Bush

There is a perception that the NCLB mandates might force educators to focus so intently on the high-stake tests that they will neglect skills that are ultimately more important for a well-rounded education, such as problem solving. This book suggests a more comprehensive approach to testing, in which all existing data in a district is scrutinized for potential direction for improvements.

Overall, lawmakers believe that testing will measure how much each student learns. A teacher is effective when a student learns, and many determine teaching effectiveness without establishing learning results. A teacher can give a great lesson; but if the students do not understand and retain what is being taught, then the lesson has no value.

Annual testing establishes benchmarks of student knowledge. Tests keyed to rigorous state academic standards provide a measure of student knowledge and skills. If the academic standards are truly rigorous, then student learning will be rigorous as well.

The overwhelming majority of students who drop out of school do so because they are frustrated. They cannot read or write or learn. Testing helps with the early identification of students who are having trouble learning so they may get the services they need to succeed.

Author's perspective:
Randy McDaniel discusses the role of testing and data.

Much of the debate over academic assessments revolves around whether or not current assessment data actually brings meaning to the table as educators look at student learning. One of the most pervasive myths of education is that we test too much. The reality is that we test too few of the important things along the way, and we use the results to measure things already done rather than things that still need to be done[12]. Many would argue that learning is a subjective term and, therefore, cannot be accurately measured by large-scale assessments. This may be true; however, if education is in the learning business, then it is the obligation of the educational community to come together and agree on some criteria.

Some view academic assessment as a necessary evil at best and an outright abomination at worst. Complaints (often valid) center around the testing methodology; the amount of classroom time devoted to assessments; the value of those assessments; the lag time between the assessment and the time the student scores are returned to the school; and the way the data is then interpreted. Real reform is needed to address these issues.

However, it is equally important to realize how data can be used and is used throughout most other professions. Rather than viewing data as evil or wasteful, educators might view learning data much as doctors view test results returned from the laboratory: as a place to begin to treat the malady in an informed way. All student-focused data can help paint the picture of students' current status regarding learning.

---

[12] Gary West. "Technology Tools to Make Educational Accountability Work," *T.H.E. Journal.* December 2000.

Very seldom is what the data "means" actually discussed. Instead being viewed as beginnings, assessments are often viewed as end games that merely show what was missed. Strangely, this data is not conasidered as the next events are planned. Assessments are merely "weighing events:" students are assessed (weighed), the results are tallied in some fashion, and the educational process moves on, regardless of the results.

Just as most Americans expect the medical community to stay abreast of new research findings and to incorporate new data, they should expect all educators to understand how student-focused data is collected and know its possible uses. It would seem ludicrous to imagine a doctor treating all 12-year-old patients exactly the same, regardless of their current health status and history, so why should this happen in the classroom?

A potential model for enhancing teacher use of learning data borrows heavily from the health care industry in that it requires accurate, real-time data to made diagnostic decisions. The data "informs practice," rather than actually superceding and overriding expert, field-based, and hands-on practice. The proposed model recasts educators at every level, and especially teachers, as expert diagnosticians. In this role, educators become experts at looking at various learning data and making diagnostic decisions regarding needed interventions to assist students in mastering agreed-upon curricula. The fundamental component of this model is the need for educators to have accurate, timely, and meaningful data to determine which interventions best fit the situation. As educators spot learning issues, they can intervene with appropriate steps. (These steps might include temporary reassignment to another classroom, activity, group, etc.) Educators would be looking not only at negatives, but also at positive gains in students' achievement. Therefore, students who are progressing more quickly in some areas would be better placed to take advantage of their current knowledge, whereas students who have not grasped a concept would receive additional help rather than proceeding, regardless of assessment results.

Chapter 2

Types and Sources of Data and Tests

The NCLB act emphasizes the need for accountability on behalf of the state, the school district, the teacher, the parent, and the student. It also emphasizes another important need: developing a clear understanding of both what students know and what they do not know. Only by identifying these gaps in learning can educators construct a clear understanding of which instructional strategies are effective and which are not.

Disaggregating data is one of the important means by which knowledge gaps can be identified and knowledge can be shared. Because the NCLB act requires that at least 95 percent of all applicable student groups in every school be assessed (be it in one year or an average of two or three years), educators will have access to information about a broad range of students from different groups (e.g., English language learners and special education students). Data disaggregating can identify groups of students having trouble in certain areas. (The NCLB act requires states to collect data pertaining to reading/language arts, mathematics, and science.) These students can then be exposed to the instructional strategies proven effective in best teaching these areas. In effect, data disaggregation gives educators a tool for identifying the instructional methods best suited to their students—for both topics addressed within the NCLB act and those topics offered by each district.

It is important to note that the term *data* is used in its broadest sense here. To deepen their understanding of student learning, educators should evaluate all pertinent data available, not just the data collected to create report cards for the NCLB act. This could include, but not be limited to, local learning data (the body of evidence collected daily by classroom teachers), state assessments, national assessments, norm-referenced assessments, criterion-referenced assessments, surveys, student demographics, and other

Author's perspective:
Randy McDaniel discusses data criteria.
Data gathered about student learning should meet several criteria: it should be relevant (e.g., it should be collected to ascertain whether, in fact, students have learned the intended curriculum), it should be timely (e.g., it should be given in the most time-efficient manner, and scores should be immediately available to educators and parents), and it should be informative (e.g., the data should be displayed in clear and agreed-on styles to assist with diagnosis, rather than merely to document results).

locally relevant information that can assist educators as they strive to enhance student learning.

This chapter, as well as Chapter 4, will spell out some key terms surrounding academic standards, testing, and data disaggregation. In its past benchmarking efforts, APQC has found that schools sometimes do not review test results because they can be difficult to understand. Although this book does not address how to develop tests, it does outline the key existing features of tests so that educators can understand existing data and apply it to instruction and administrational activities.

Identify Existing Data

In collecting data for interpretation and disaggregation, educators should begin by conducting a data audit to learn what data the district or school already possesses. There is so much more than standardized test results that can be taken into account for a balanced perspective. It is important to realize that most, if not all, of the information required is already out there. The key is to find and disseminate it. Places to begin include teachers' student files and school, district, and board member offices.

A summary of data for identification that states and districts commonly collect follows.

- Grade level
- Individual student test scores
- Low-income and limited English proficiency
- Number of absent or exempt students

- Required data and their formats
- Student exemptions by reason
- Student special education status
- Student-level test score data
- Total campus enrollment

Other data that may exist at school and district levels follows.

- **Information about the students**—whether the student has ever been referred to special education courses; drop-out, attendance, and graduation rates; health issues/handicaps; mobility rates; suspensions and tardy rates; SAT/ACT scores; percentage of students promoted to the next grade; hours of homework per week; percentage of students who go on to a four-year college; percentage of students who receive an A or B average; extracurricular activities; credits earned; exit exam results; guidance records; disciplinary action records; student follow-up surveys; college entrance exam scores; postsecondary enrollment records; and postsecondary transcript data

- **Information about the school**—safety records, physical plan, image in the community, support services for students and teachers, number/experience of teachers and administrators, race/gender of teachers and administrators, teacher certification, student-teacher ratios, administrator-teacher ratios, teacher-turnover rates, teacher salaries and trends, schedules, support staff, course offerings, course enrollments and levels, per-pupil spending, number of students per computer, occupational competency test results, work-readiness assessments, teacher evaluations, personnel files, staff development activities, continuing education credits, in-service records, records on tutorial programs, information collected for purposes of applying or responding to grantors, and pervious evaluations of classroom and programs

- **Information about the parents**—parents' income levels, education, and employment; the number of families on public assistance or free and reduced lunch; parental satisfaction survey data; and percentage of parents who attend parent-teacher conferences

- **Information about the school district**—description of district and history; number of schools, students, teachers, and administrators; teacher mobility/turnover; and support services for students and teachers
- **Information about the community**—description of the population, housing trends and demographic shifts, health issues, crime rate, key employers, economic base, and community survey results
- **Information about the state**—state assessments, statewide test scores administration, scoring timelines, population, race/ethnicity, and socioeconomic status

The first step is to investigate what data is available. The more teachers know about their students, the more they can appropriately adapt the curriculum to those students' learning needs.

Next, it is important to select the data that is valued. Simply collecting numbers will not necessarily provide useful information about students' needs. When it comes to pulling data about students' abilities, it is critical to determine which students do not meet reading, math, or science standards and what factors are correlated with students not meeting these standards. For instance, if students' performance in fifth grade science varies by race, what other factors in the classrooms are differentiating instruction among the student groups? The nature of a question often determines the next steps in data collection and analysis, which, in this case, is determining what can be done to help the groups of students failing to meet content standards[13].

The most helpful data sources are often those that are most frequently reported. Capturing trends and tracking tests for specific patterns of performance allows educators to make a preemptive strike against problematic areas and to help students who are falling behind. This is where the collection of assessment data, progress reports, and other frequent measures of performance can lead to success.

---

[13] Annenberg Institute for School Reform. *Using Data for School Improvement.* 1998.

Data sources may represent attainment or gains[14]. A student's level of attainment is measured by determining whether the student has achieved a specified level of skill, knowledge, or ability. Measuring gains, on the other hand, looks at whether a student's achievements have improved over time. Measuring only attainment provides only partial information about performance at a school and can lead to false conclusions and poor decisions. For example, educators might note that a student has attained a score of 78 percent on a geometry test, but without knowing that the student attained a score of 64 percent on a geometry test taken six months ago, they would have no way of knowing that the student had made significant gains. Educators who look only at attainment might be inclined to change instructional strategies that are actually working. Educators who look at both attainment and gain indicators can have a more complete picture of how their students are performing.

A note on anecdotal data sources[15]: Casual observations and informal comments from parents or students can be helpful; however, it is important to take anecdotal evidence into account only within the context of additional perspectives. Individual comments may not represent the ideas of the community as a whole, so it is important to determine an appropriate number of people to approach on an issue and to select a random sample. This will later extend to the entire continuous improvement effort. One of the mandates of the NCLB act is to use proven reform methods. For example, a principal would not initiate a reading program simply based on anecdotal evidence, without first investigating local need and proven results.

Deciding Which Data to Use

All stakeholders should provide input on what data matters most, based on agreed-upon goals. Obviously, the more data (that is, valid and relevant data) an educator has, the more informed his/her

---

[14] Bradby, Denise, Karen Levesque, Kristi Rossi, and Peter Teitelbaum. *At Your Fingertips: Using Everyday Data to Improve Schools.* MPR Associates Inc., 1998.
[15] Bradby, Denise, Karen Levesque, Kristi Rossi, and Peter Teitelbaum. *At Your Fingertips: Using Everyday Data to Improve Schools.* MPR Associates Inc., 1998.

decisions will be. An appropriate accumulation of data will ensure that educators resist the temptation to make significant decisions based on a single test score and provide context for test scores. Bringing in representatives from all major stakeholders will also ensure alignment between what data is gathered and what data is actually used. This is a collaborative process that will involve group conversations.

A tool in selecting what data to focus on is to break data down into three broad categories: input variables, process variables, and outcome variables[16]. By understanding the input + process = outcome equation, educations can more easily understand how data affects goals (and hence, what data to focus on).

- **Input variables** are what students, teachers, administrators, and community members bring to the table; they include the cultural and educational background, knowledge, and socioeconomic status of students and the level of education or previous in-service training experiences of teachers.

- **Process variables** are the processes currently being used, such as the instructional techniques, materials, and the levels of teacher and parent participation in decision making.

- **Outcome variables** are the results of input and process variables; they include student tests, observation data, and survey results.

An example of an outcome variable is that a student achieves a high score on the SAT and is invited to attend a prestigious university. Input and process variables contributing to the student's success would include the knowledge, experience, and dedication of her teachers, the student's desire to succeed, parental support, and strong instructional support in language arts and mathematics. This section's side bar lists additional examples of school inputs, process variables, and outcome variables[17].

The key is for stakeholders to detail district, campus, classroom, and individual goals to see what data should be leveraged to support

[16] American Association of School Administrators (www.aasa.org)

[17] Bradby, Denise, Karen Levesque, Kristi Rossi, and Peter Teitelbaum. *At Your Fingertips: Using Everyday Data to Improve Schools.* MPR Associates Inc., 1998.

those goals. At each level, stakeholders can identify the overall purpose and expectations of students and staff. This most likely has already been determined by a campus or district, in terms of what is expected of students, teachers, and all educators.

Because data reveals only results and issues—and not solutions—stakeholders can then determine how data can be used to bolster each goal and support students and staff in meeting expectations. This process is detailed in Chapter 5.

Inputs from Students
- The students' current knowledge and abilities
- Native language spoken at home
- Economic advantages/disadvantages
- Students' interests

Inputs from Teachers
- Teachers' knowledge and skills
- Teachers' qualifications
- Student-teacher ratio
- Teachers' experience

Inputs from the Community
- Community values
- Parent involvement
- School volunteers
- Business donations
- Business involvement in work-based learning

Physical Plan, Equipment, and Budget Inputs
- Characteristics and size of the school campus
- Amount and quality of equipment and technology
- School budget
- Per-pupil expenditures
- Length of school day
- Length of school year
- Length of class time

Process Variables

- Curriculum frameworks
- Integration across academic disciplines
- English/language arts instruction (e.g., the writing process, reading approaches, and phonic instruction)
- Teaching diverse populations (e.g., high expectations for all students, immersion/ESL/bilingual students, multicultural education, and multiple intelligence approaches)
- Instructional materials (e.g., textbooks and resources and instructional tools such as computers)
- Pedagogical approaches (e.g., active learning, teacher-directed instruction, and small-group instruction),
- School-to-work approach (e.g., use of technology, work-based learning experiences, and career guidance)
- Assessment methodologies (e.g., essays, portfolios, lab assignments, projects, performance tasks, rubrics, and short-answer testing)
- Supporting structures (e.g., teacher training, block scheduling, teacher planning time, number of course hours/periods per week assigned to teachers, class size, and support for administrators and teachers)

School Output Variables

- Academic knowledge and cognitive skills (e.g., students' academic achievement and critical thinking skills)
- Social development (e.g., self-confidence, motivation, and interpersonal skills)
- Completing high school
- Preparedness for employment (e.g., ability to solve real-world problems, computer literacy, work-readiness skills, and attainment of industry skill certification)
- Success after high school (e.g. students' ability to meet college eligibility requirements, successful college career, and successful employment)

A Problematic but Helpful Data Source: Surveys

Surveys are a tricky source for relevant and valid data. It is often true that surveys yield the answers we expect, rather than new information, because of the nature of the questions we ask.

Understanding Validity and Reliability

An assessment is considered valid if it measures what it is supposed to measure (that is, if it measures the content standards). Data is also considered valid if inferences and actions made on the basis of test scores are accurate and appropriate. A valid standards-based assessment is aligned with the intended learning and knowledge to be measured and provides an accurate and reliable measurement of students' achievement relative to the standard. This means that an educator should be certain that a student taking an eighth-grade math test is being tested on eighth-grade standards. A high score on the test should indicate proficiency in the eighth-grade content standards.

Reliability is the degree to which the results of an assessment are dependable and consistently measure a student's knowledge and skills. Reliability indicates the consistency of scores across different tasks or items that measure the same skill, across raters, and over time. Thus, reliability is the relationship between test items intended to measure the same learning or knowledge (item reliability), the relationship between two administrations of the same test to the same students (test/retest reliability), or the degree of agreement across two graders (grader reliability).

Consequently, many districts are turning to professional vendors to support survey development. These surveys do not ask questions that test results may already indicate, such as a weakness in a certain subject, but instead ask questions to determine why test results are as they are. For instance, a school district can survey teachers to determine how easily they can access relevant data for curriculum development, what troubles they are having implementing certain processes in the classroom, and what information they need from teachers in earlier grades on other campuses. Additionally, a district could survey students to determine whether they know what is expected of them in specific subjects, know what their test results are, and know what to do to improve them. Data collected from such a survey could be used to adapt approaches to curriculum and instruction.

When done correctly, surveys can be used to address hurdles, barriers, and supports so that educators can identify what is helping students reach goals. Some helpful guidelines on surveys follow.

The National Center for Education Statistics collects and reports information on the academic performance of the nation's students, as well as general information on the condition of public and private education. According to the NCES, the users of data must be able to understand both its benefits and its limitations. When survey data is evaluated statistically, a systematic assessment of all sources of error for key statistics that will be studied or reported should be conducted. According to the statistical standards developed by the National Center for Educational Statistics, a survey evaluation should:

- identify the range of potential sources of error;
- provide for the measurement of the magnitude of sampling error and sources of the various types of non-sampling errors expected to be a problem;
- include studies to determine what factors are associated with differential levels of error and assess procedures for reducing the magnitude of these errors;
- assess the quality of the final estimates, including comparisons to external sources and where possible, comparisons to prior estimates from the same data collection; and
- include a technical report or series of technical reports summarizing results of evaluation studies (for example, a quality profile or total survey error model).

If their survey data fits the criteria developed by NCES, educators should consider including it in their data analysis. The NCES specifies that educators should review past surveys similar to the one being planned to determine what statistical evaluation data has been collected in prior surveys. They should also look for any potential problems that may affect the magnitude of error. Again, the greater the significance of the survey results, the greater is the need to seek assistance from a professional vendor or survey expert.

Who Pulls This Data?

Although all educators are responsible for recognizing key terms in disaggregating data so they can leverage data appropriately, there are some specific roles involved in making data disaggregation possible on campus.

It is traditionally the task of the central office of a district or school to pull data and make it available to teachers. Teachers should not be expected to search for each piece of data they need. Instead, the central office should develop a procedure for individual student assessment data to be easily retrievable by individual teachers and for aggregate student assessment data to be retrievable by district administrators and teachers. It should also train individual teachers and administrators in student-assessment data retrieval. By tasking the central office with creating a system to regularly pull such data, a district or school can have a consistent policy on what information needs to be provided by each educator.

The central office can also ensure that data is used to correct the system and not to punish educators for specific performance results. Punishment will only encourage data hoarding. Teachers must see that data is used to focus attention on learning and improving education, not just to categorize classes and schools. They can be assured that data will be thoughtfully and consistently used in an evaluation and that they will review their class data only in comparison to a group and not to other specific teachers. A school's culture will not be conducive to data-driven decision making if the members of that culture continually step on each others' toes. The central office can help board members, district staff, principals, and teachers understand their common purpose and the important individual roles in the data system.

The central office should identify which elements of student assessments should be analyzed to promote individual student achievement and, in aggregate form, to promote program achievement. It should establish a procedure for reviewing performance results to determine whether core subject achievement has increased at each grade level in each building of the district. It should review all student achievement data and develop instructional, curricular, and assessment strategies that address students' learning needs coming out of the data analysis. The central office can then share this data with all educators and create strategies that will address areas where student achievement can be increased. The central office role should be one of service and support, including providing materials, staff development, and resources for extended day activities.

The district's central office should also take responsibility for:

- managing the development of data disaggregation processes and systems, including setting priorities, coordinating, and reporting group activities;
- determining system requirements in conjunction with user district offices, schools, and staff;
- determining and designing an approach to implement user requirements using an application development tool in conjunction with data and functionality resident in student information systems; and
- developing technology solutions considering present operational systems and standard software systems.

The U.S. Department of Education's 2003 report *Innovation Guide: Public School Choice* by Edvance and WestEd described how one district's central office provided its principals with data.

> *In August, all principals receive a report with disaggregated data. The report breaks down student performance by race, ethnicity, gender, and grade level. The principal knows the percentages of students who are performing at, above, and below grade level. They receive a '20-20' report that breaks out the lowest 20 percent, the highest 20 percent, and the middle 20 percent. This data is used to help indicate which students need additional help and which need specific assistance (e.g., concerning math or reading) to get them over the bar. Some principals use the data to group students together in an effort to provide very intense and specific instruction in a certain subject area.*

Central office administrators should play an active role in facilitating educational success. Administrators specializing in curriculum and instruction should visit classrooms and campuses frequently in order to learn what teachers and principals need in terms of resources and support. Instructional supervisors with subject matter expertise can share best practices. An important and new role for most administrators is taking responsibility for gathering and disseminating data, as well as coordinating the review and time set to solve problems. Administrators need to facilitate problem solving. This involves assessing the data disaggregation staff's ability to respond to a customer's request, to recommend improvements in standardized testing evaluation capabilities, to evaluate participation in the data disaggregation program, and to market the program to all stakeholders. This requires a substantial commitment and vision from a key administrator, such as the superintendent or director of curriculum and instruction. It is beneficial for this same key figure to ensure that goals are set and met. He or she should work with district faculty, staff, and parents and community stakeholders to craft plans for meeting goals by certain dates and lays the tracks for clear, steady progress. Most activities will involve the same staff managing and carrying out tasks. Long-term goals are reached through incremental improvements. Instead of setting an inordinate number of goals, priorities should be set by academic standards for small, manageable achievements along the way.

The superintendent and school board share leadership of the district's data efforts but play significantly different roles[18]. The board typically adopts policies to govern the system, whereas the superintendent manages daily operations. To make effective policy decisions, the board must understand data. For example, the board needs to know that some data trends are the result of a common cause (a regular feature of the school system, such as normal student attendance patterns), and some are the result of a special cause (an unusual circumstance, such as a flu bug that causes students to miss school on a big test day). Otherwise, the district might spend an inappropriate amount of time trying to solve a problem that was a

---

[18] Bradby, Denise, Karen Levesque, Kristi Rossi, and Peter Teitelbaum. *At Your Fingertips: Using Everyday Data to Improve Schools*. MPR Associates Inc., 1998.

fluke. The superintendent's role is to empower central office and school staff to use data as effectively as possible to meet the board's mandates. Therefore, the superintendent translates the board's vision for the school district into measurable goals backed with data[19].

Principals are responsible for simplifying school improvement planning and involving all educators in data analysis and goal setting. They should work as a team and provide tools and procedures to allow teachers and students to work as teams. An important role for principals is also to demystify and promote a regard for state standards and standardized tests. Although principals bear ultimate responsibility for what happens in their schools, they must work with teachers to use data in ways to best serve their unique student populations and school needs.

Reviewing Academic Content and Achievement Standards and Standardized Tests

It is also important to collect as much information as is available concerning state guidelines. Teachers and administrators are responsible for knowing their states' guidelines, and it is absolutely critical to become well versed in the state standards at whatever level of detail can be attained.

Although the Department of Education does not dictate the content of each state's academic standards, the federal government does provide guidelines for states to use as they develop academic content standards. According to those guidelines, academic content standards should:
- specify what students are expected to know and be able to do;
- contain coherent and rigorous content;
- encourage the teaching of advanced learning;
- be clear and specific;
- give teachers, students, and parents sufficient direction to guide teaching and learning;
- be understandable so that educators can teach the expected content;

---

[19] Bradby, Denise, Karen Levesque, Kristi Rossi, and Peter Teitelbaum. *At Your Fingertips: Using Everyday Data to Improve Schools.* MPR Associates Inc., 1998.

- be attainable by students; and
- be written in clear, jargon-free, and straightforward prose accessible to a wide range of audiences.

The federal government also specifies that academic achievement standards explicitly define what students should know and be able to do to demonstrate proficiency on assessments. These achievement standards should include achievement levels, achievement descriptors (competencies associated with each achievement level), exemplars (examples of student work that illustrate the range of achievement), and cut scores (scores on an assessment that separate one level of achievement from another).

Some states have very specific guidelines, whereas other state's guidelines are very general. One state might simply note that second graders are required to be able to multiply. Another state might require second graders to multiple two numbers by three numbers, with the numbers presented in a single line.

To effectively manage instruction, a school district should also have a thorough knowledge of its state's assessment. Educators should know how the state will test students. Obviously teachers cannot be provided with the test before it is given; but they should know how subjects will be broached and in what format students should be familiar with answering questions. For example, teachers should be sure that students are familiar with multiple-choice tests as well as open-ended responses if both will occur on a state test.

To understand how standards are aligned with assessments, educators should seek all available support material from the state that details characteristics of its guidelines. This will allow educators to ensure that content and performance match. These characteristics will detail:

- **Comprehensiveness**—What range of standards will be tested?
- **Emphasis**—What degree of emphasis is expected on each standard, and how does that emphasis vary among subjects?
- **Depth**—What is the cognitive demand and depth of the tandards?

Types of Assessment

This section includes descriptions of commonly used tests so that educators may use a similar vocabulary when discussing and examining test results. These definitions may also be useful in explaining test results to parents and the community.

A state may use either criterion-referenced assessments or augmented norm-referenced assessments. States that use a norm-referenced assessment must augment the test with additional items as necessary to accurately measure the state's academic content standards, and the assessment must express students' results in terms of the state's academic achievement standards.

Criterion-referenced assessments are intended to measure how well a student has learned a specific body of knowledge and skills. In these tests, a student's performance is compared to a specific learning objective or achievement standard rather than to the performance of other students. It is possible that all of the students tested will reach a particular goal or achievement standard. Results for these exams, which include advanced placement exams, are often presented as "85 percent of students met or exceeded the standards." The Sunshine State Standards portion of the Florida Comprehensive Assessment Test (FCAT) is an example of a criterion-referenced test.

Figure 2 presents an example of the type of report Florida provides regarding results of its criterion-referenced assessment in reading. Note that the data from criterion-referenced tests can be broken down by content—words/phrases, main idea/purpose, comparisons, reference/research—giving educators performance results of how students are performing in specific content areas.

In **norm-referenced assessment,** a student's performance is compared to the performance of a larger group, usually a national sample representing a wide and diverse cross-section of students. The main goal of a norm-referenced test is to classify students. These tests highlight achievement differences between and among students to produce a rank order of students from high to low achievers. Results of norm-referenced tests are often presented as "students scored in the 85th percentile," meaning that they scored higher than 84 percent of the students who took the test. The Iowa Test of Basic

Grade	District Number	District Name	School Name	Number of Students	Mean Developmental Scale Score	Mean Scale Score (100-500)	\% in each Achievement level 1	2	3	4	5	Words/Phrases	Main Idea/Purpose	Comparisons	Reference/Research
State Report of District Results - Grade 5, Reading												**Mean Points Earned by Content**			
Number of Points Possible												11	20	10	4
5	00	Statewide	Grade 5	188, 107	1290	298	23	15	33	25	5	7	13	6	3
5	05	Spring	Van Buren	150	1411	318	15	8	34	34	8	8	14	7	3
5	05	Spring	Kennedy	252	1418	319	13	12	34	30	11	8	14	7	3
5	05	Spring	Riverside	80	1124	271	34	21	32	13	0	6	11	5	2
5	05	Spring	Jackson	97	1226	288	29	14	35	22	0	7	12	6	3
5	05	Spring	Sunnydale	72	1368	311	16	14	34	30	5	8	13	6	3

Figure 2

Skills and the Stanford 9 are examples of norm-referenced assessments.

These assessments are normed using a representative group of students who are given the test prior to its availability to the public.

The scores of the students who take the test after publication are then compared to those of the norm group. Tests such as the California Achievement Test and the Iowa Test of Basic Skills are normed using a national sample of students. Norming a test is a complex and costly process, so test preparers typically use norms for seven years. All students who take the test during that seven year period have their scores compared to the original norm group.

Figure 3 shows one student's results from a Stanford 9 test. The "No. of Items" column tells how many items the student was tested on (a total of 84 items for reading, for example). The "Raw Score" is the number of items the student answered correctly (71 for reading). The "Scaled Score" is based on a factor that weights scores according to their difficulty, giving more weight to hard questions and less weight to easier questions. The "National Percentile Rank score" (National PR-S) provides two pieces of information: the number before the hyphen tells the student's position in relation to his or her peers; for example, a score of 78 tells that a student scored higher than 77 percent of students taking the test. The number after the hyphen is the stanine score. A stanine score of 1 to 3 is below average, of 4 to 6 is average, and of 7 to 9 is above average. The

Subsets and Totals	Number of Items	Raw Score	Scaled Score	National PR-S	National NCE
Total Reading	84	71	671	78-7	66.3
Vocabulary	30	27	678	78-7	66.3
Reading Comprehension	54	44	668	75-6	64.2
Total Mathematics	78	68	676	90-8	77.0
Problem Solving	48	41	669	87-7	73.7
Proceedures	30	27	686	87-7	73.7
Languages	48	29	621	43-5	46.3
Prewriting	24	19	656	73-6	62.9
Composing	24	20	629	54-5	52.1
Editing	24	10	590	20-3	32.3

Figure 3

National NCE is a version of the National PR-S that is used to make comparisons across individual tests.

State assessments are typically criterion-referenced because the standards do not waiver. With norm-referenced tests, a bar of what is average would improve with students' performance; there is no way that more than 50 percent of the students can be above average. Some states compromise through augmented norm-referenced assessment.

Students with disabilities who are unable to participate in a regular assessment are given an **alternative assessment,** based on the circumstance. The most common allowance is an extension of time to take a standardized test, although it may also involve adjusted questions or a different approach to taking the test (e.g., vocally). This assessment must be aligned with the state's content and student-achievement standards, must report student achievement with the same frequency and level of detail as the state's regular assessment, and must serve the same purpose as the assessment for which it is an alternate. (On a local scale, alternative assessments can be used to determine how students perform on subjects not traditionally measured through standardized tests, such as painting or soccer, as well as how students perform on core topics such as reading using alternative approaches.)

There are also a number of common tests created at the local level. Examples follow.

In **performance tests,** students demonstrate their abilities through such works as presentations or portfolios.

Formative assessment takes place at several points during a teaching or learning phase. Information gained from this type of assessment is used to guide further teaching or learning steps. Formative assessments can include questioning, commenting on a presentation, or writing.

Maximum performance tests include tests of intelligence, aptitude (prediction of future level of performance), and achievement (an evaluation of present levels of knowledge, skills, or competence). At least three determinants are involved in every score on tests of maximum performance: innate ability, environment influences (including education), and motivation. There is no way to determine how much of a student's score is caused by any one of these three determinants.

Tests can also be classified according to the types of questions asked. **Simple** test questions ask students to recall and use knowledge. For example, such questions might ask a language arts student to tell the plot of a story or a social studies student to list the causes of the Great Depression. Although these questions are important to test student's knowledge retention, they should not be the only questions asked of students on tests. **Complex** test questions require more complex critical thinking skills, such as analyzing, predicting, comparing and contrasting, classifying, analyzing perspectives, and making inductions and deductions. Examples of these types of questions include predicting what might happen next in a story or considering how the Great Depression might have been prevented.

The form of the response is another way that tests are classified. **Objective tests** include items, such as multiple choice, whose answers are either correct or incorrect. **Subjective tests** include items that will be scored using some personal judgment. Tests can also be classified as select-response/supply-response (select-response items, such as multiple-choice, ask students to choose the correct response from a list of options vs. supply-response items, which ask students to provide the correct response), written/oral performance tests, standardized/informal tests, tests of speed/power, group/individual tests, or verbal/nonverbal tests[20].

Assessment Reporting: State Report Cards

A great resource for succinctly reviewing assessment results is the federally mandated state report card. According to the NCLB act, each district and school receiving Title I, Part A funds must provide a report card annually outlining its students' achievements. The assessments used must be aligned with the state's content standards, be consistent with nationally recognized professional and technical standards, be used in a valid and reliable manner (see page 3 for the definition of *valid* and *reliable*), and test higher order thinking skills using multiple measures.

---

[20] Howard B. Lyman. *Test Scores and What They Mean.* Allyn and Bacon, 1998.

To be certain that highly confidential test data is not seen by the wrong person, schools should include security measures, such as passwords, to ensure only those authorized will have access to the test data. Access could be determined so that users will have access to data at the appropriate levels. For example, district personnel might have access to reports for all the schools in their district, whereas teachers might have access only to reports for their school or classroom.

Annual state report cards are broken down by:

- gender,
- race/ethnicity (American Indian or Alaskan, Black, Asian or Pacific Islander, Hispanic, White, Multiracial, or no valid information),
- special education (with or without accommodations),
- general education (with or without accommodations),
- free or reduced-price meal eligibility,
- English language learner (whose chance of success in an English-only classroom is below that of peers or comparable ability who have English as their primary language), and
- migrant student (who has moved within a designated period from one district to another so that the parents could obtain temporary or seasonal employment in agriculture as their principle means of livelihood).

Administration-level information may include school name, grade, test date, and total student count, end-of-course examination passing rate, attendance rate, dropout rate, high school completion rate, and percentage of students completing advanced courses, SAT and ACT examination participation and results, school and district staff, finances, programs, and demographics.

State report cards include the following information for each state:

- state assessment results by performance level, including two-year trend data for each subject and grade tested,
- a comparison between annual objectives and actual performance for each student group,
- the percentage of each group of students not tested,

- graduation rates for secondary school students and any other student achievement indicators that the state chooses,
- performance of school districts on adequate yearly progress including the number and names of schools identified as needing improvement, and
- professional qualifications of teachers in the state, including the percentage of teachers in the classroom with only emergency or provisional credentials and the percentage of classes in the state that are not taught by highly qualified teachers, including a comparison between high- and low-income schools.

Under the NCLB act, states must build on their existing yearly academic assessments, which produce individual student interpretive, descriptive, and diagnostic reports. States' reports must provide information for each student regarding his or her achievement on academic assessments that are aligned to the state's academic content and achievement standards.

An individual student report must have the following characteristics:

- provide valid and reliable information for each student on the academic content and achievement standards expected of all students;
- display this information in a format and language that is understandable to parents, teachers, and principals;
- deliver these reports as soon as possible after the assessment is administered; and
- provide detailed information on student achievement to the level that maintains the validity and reliability of the assessment.

Chapter 3 will detail how to break down data using technology support, and Chapter 4 will detail how to analyze data in order to apply it to improve student performance.

Chapter 3

How to Break Down Data: Technology Support

After determining what data exists and then collecting it, the next step is to break it down in order to understand it. First, data should be entered into a computerized database. Doing so makes it easy to organize the data and to recognize statistically significant trends. Spreadsheet programs can easily calculate an average deviation, variance, and a standard deviation for any group; however, it is still important for educators to examine test results and other data. Even though there may not always be a need to initiate a relevant statistical analysis, it is important for educators to be able to understand the results.

By answering five common questions, this chapter will address the role of technology in data-driven decision-making in education and common mistakes to avoid.

What technology support options does my school need?

"Technology support" refers specifically to the infrastructure in place in K-12 education that stores, sorts, and allows manipulation of student learning data. This infrastructure includes necessary hardware and software, staff development and training, and technology support staff. Within this narrow field of technology support, computer-aided instruction (CAI), computer-managed instruction (CMI), or any other instructional software is not being addressed. Rather, the intent is to focus on how technology can assist educators in better understanding how, and to what extent, their students have learned the school's curriculum. This focus saves an extraordinary amount of effort and expense in "wiring schools" with networks. However, it must be said that without a networking infrastructure or modern hardware and software, many of the abilities to use the data stored in educational institutions will be unavailable to practitioners.

Technology support in K-12 education is an area that leaves much to be desired. Many teachers and principals are awaiting delivery on the promise of technology. Specifically, technology support fails to deliver quality assistance that meets the needs of educators. Educators have huge amounts of data, as identified in Chapter 2, but many remain information poor because of the lack of a comprehensive plan for how to accumulate, disaggregate, and leverage existing data. More importantly, a meaningful methodology of making diagnostic decisions is seldom in place to effectively make use of the data. In his article, "Technology Tools to Make Educational Accountability Work," Gary West noted, "Without a comprehensive technology support plan, it will be extremely difficult to use real-time data to make decisions[21]."

To better understand the differences between the current status of technology support in education and the ideal status, we need a firm grasp of the goal—to provide educators with the necessary tools, equipment, and training to make timely, educationally sound decisions to track (and ultimately) increase student learning. According to researchers Amy Ronnkvist, Sara L. Dexter, and Ronald E. Anderson (2000), "Technology support in America's schools typically comprises access to equipment, dedicated staff, and professional development programming. ...This support is profoundly resource dependent[22]." Their research highlighted the pronounced effect on use when the technology support was designed with the instructional needs of teachers in mind (i.e., creating convenient access to necessary resources, providing individualized support, training teachers to integrate technology into the classroom, and providing resources as incentives). It is key that

---

[21] West, Gary. "Technology Tools to Make Educational Accountability Work." *THE Journal*, December 2002.

[22] Anderson, Ronald E., Sara L. Dexter, and Amy Ronnkvist. "Technology Support: Its Depth, Breadth, and Impact in American Schools." Center for Research on Information Technology and Organization, University of California at Irvine and the University of Minnesota, 2000

leaders in education first assess the current status and then make plans to address areas of needs.

There are many methods by which a school can determine its current and needed level of technology support. One notable example was developed by the International Society for Technology in Education (ISTE). The Technology Support Index (TSI) assessment is a tool for schools and districts to profile their technology support programs and to provide solutions based on those unique profiles. The TSI was developed by Chip Kimball on behalf of ISTE and the Bill and Melinda Gates Foundation. (See appendix.)

The TSI assessment contains four domains of support:
1. equipment standards,
2. staffing and processes,
3. professional development, and
4. intelligent systems.

The TSI was developed so that four general stages describe the school's or district's capability for each strategy and also for each overall domain. The four stages of capability are: emergent, islands, integrated, and exemplary. Schools can use the TSI to profile their current technology support status and use the resulting profile as a catalyst for planning.

Technology support is a fundamental component of data-driven decision making. Support for technology in education is a less glamorous feature of technology in education. However, much like a building must have a well-designed and well-built foundation to be structurally sound, without a strong commitment to a highly effective implementation of support for technology, the promise of technology cannot be realized by educators.

What should my district's technology solution look like?

Technology solutions are designed to resolve complex problems, so they should address both the technological component (e.g., hardware, software, and user interface) and the human component (e.g., training, staff development, ease of use, and responsiveness to individual needs). Technology solutions must be both extremely powerful and robust on one hand and easy enough to master in order to get meaningful data quickly on the other. The ideal solutions required to assist educators in dealing with large amounts of student learning data would have the following components:

- the ability to store, sort, aggregate, and disaggregate student demographic information (e.g., gender, ethnicity, socioeconomic status, migrant status, special education or disability status, federal program status, and language proficiency)
- the ability to store, sort, aggregate, and disaggregate student learning data (e.g., formal state and/or national assessments and locally gathered data from teacher grade books)
- the ability to store, sort, aggregate, and disaggregate other key student information (e.g., attendance, graduation, and dropout rates)
- the ability to store and manage the school's curriculum (e.g., local, state, and national standards, the alignment of local curriculum to state and national standards, the alignment of local curriculum between grades and courses, the design of curriculum-based lessons and units, and curriculum-based course syllabi and weekly plans)
- the ability to do query-based reporting (based on locally determined criteria)
- the ability to store and retrieve data collected over time (longitudinal reports of subgroups or individual students based on user-entered criteria)
- the ability to store and retrieve diagnostic assessment items correlated to the school's curriculum (e.g., lessons, units, or other activities that specifically address a particular learning outcome)
- the ability to store and retrieve "benchmark assessments" that track a task or series of tasks that has consistent protocols for a targeted groups of students to follow (These procedures [time frame, directions, and the task itself] are identical for each student so that educators can analyze the findings and make comparisons. This analysis can be used to determine the specific progress or regress students have made in relation to the

demonstration of targeted skills and/or retention of factual information.)

- the ability to store, sort, aggregate, and disaggregate standardized test scores (such as state and national assessments)
- the ability to store, sort, aggregate, and disaggregate the local body of evidence of student learning data (typically within a teacher's grade book). The teacher's grade book must be designed in such a way as to address traditional evaluation of learning (e.g., grades) and more authentic curriculum-based tracking of learning within the same grade book. The grade book should be powerful and flexible enough to encompass the myriad of grading methodologies found in classrooms across America.
- the ability to store, sort, aggregate, and disaggregate the local body of evidence at the classroom, building, and district level without additional complexity (The hardware and software solution must be able to collect student-learning data and have that data available to appropriate stakeholders in real time. This feature allows educators at all levels in the organization to gather and analyze student learning data that can then be used to alter the next phase(s) in the learning process [either one student at a time or using grouping alternatives]. Additionally, the solution must allow for longitudinal reports that track student learning data over time.)
- the ability to store, sort, aggregate, disaggregate, and report the entire body of evidence of student learning (This function assists educators as they collect and analyze and eventually report the findings to accreditation organizations, state departments of education, and the federal education agencies.)

According to John Bailey, director of the Office of Instructional Technology for the U. S. Department of Education, "It's almost impossible to enact NCLB without technology." The extent of data disaggregation needed to meet all NCLB criteria makes a student learning data system an imperative.

What is the ideal system for my school district, and what can we get by with?

The ideal data-driven decision-making solution is comprehensive enough to address current needs and flexible enough to grow as needs change. However, given the difficult budgetary positions of most educational institutions, it may be prudent to find a solution that has a lower-cost entry point or addresses only part of the desired goal. Districts could then add other components later as budgets permit.

To determine the ideal solution for a particular campus/district, three sets of questions (in addition to the questions posed throughout this chapter) should be addressed. First, educators should determine what data should be collected and why. Second, educators should know the current status of the district's technology infrastructure and capacity and understand how well it might eventually match with a commercial software package. Third, educators should evaluate software issues.

Data Issues
- Has the district determined what data should be collected?
- Is the local curriculum in place, and is there a process to continually update the curriculum?
- Who should have access to the data?
- How will data first get entered into the solution?
- Do we need to house the data or should it be housed by a third-party vendor?
- What internal support is needed initially, and who will support the data over time?

Hardware Issues
- Do we have an infrastructure in place to support a network or Web-based solution?
- What server requirements are needed to deliver data quickly to the users?
- Is the data secure? Are there sophisticated tools to maintain high levels of secure access and data encryption methods to protect data and meet FERPA regulations?

Software Issues

- Is the software an enterprise solution? Is the data housed in a master database that continually updates based on district use?
- Is the software browser-based for anywhere/anytime access? (If so, there are no applications to install on each workstation.)
- Does the solution have a powerful database designed to allow for data analysis? (At a minimum, the system must be relational and should handle queries across all data elements to ensure a maximum amount of flexibility.)
- Does the solution meet instructional management system (IMS) criteria? (An IMS should be able to create, store, and share best practice throughout the educational community of a campus/district.)
- Does the solution have a straightforward design? The user interface should be intuitive and result in a relatively small amount of training needed to use the system.
- What technical support is available? What are the annual costs for this support and software upgrades?

At a minimum, the decision-making group should visit multiple customers of all vendors that pass an initial screening. By visiting educators that have used the software, a school can begin to get a true picture of how the solution has helped the educators use data to make decisions.

Should a district create its own "in-house" solution?

Determining whether to create a custom in-house solution rather than purchasing a solution from a vendor requires school leaders to answer many questions. Chief among them regards the technological expertise available in the district. Many small districts simply do not have the expertise to develop, maintain, and support a sophisticated hardware and software solution. However, campuses/districts that do have the technological expertise might choose to develop an in-house solution because it allows them to have full control over its exact specifications. For the purpose of this discussion, an "in-house" solution is one that is designed, developed, supported, and maintained primarily by campus/district personnel (as opposed to purchasing a solution provided by a software vendor). Key questions that must be addressed before choosing between an in-house solution and a vendor-purchased application include:

- Does the campus/district have a true vision for the specific solution desired?
- Have professional accountant and budgetary rules been used to accurately assess the true "cost of ownership" of an in-house solution vs. a vendor purchased application?
- Does the campus/district have staff with the software programming skills needed to develop and support the vision? If so, will appropriate amounts of time be devoted to allow staff to develop the solution?
- If staff with software programming skills does exist, is there duplication of skills? For example, what if there is only one person with the required skills? Does this put the campus/district in peril if the person should leave the district?
- Does the district have the necessary hardware and software on hand (or the funds to purchase it) to support the desired solution?
- If developed in-house, are there staff development resources available to appropriately train and support the solution over time?

There are many lessons to be learned from districts that have forged ahead using data to make decisions. Key among these is to "start where you are." The temptation to want to catch up or copy a supposedly exemplary school district is difficult to avoid. However, to move an organization (especially a conservative one such as a school district) too fast is often disastrous. A better plan is to honestly assess the staff's current strengths and weaknesses and to make a specific plan to incorporate professional development to move toward the desired goal. It is unrealistic to think educators will become experts at data-driven decision making overnight or without appropriate and consistent training. Therefore, a plan for ongoing staff development must be part of all strategic plans.

Districts would also be wise to include all stakeholders in the decision-making process. Long before any funds are spent on hardware and software solutions, representatives from the various groups in the school population should determine what data they feel is most beneficial to collect and how that data can be used immediately to improve student performance. Key advice would be to start with core items that are well established in the school and to analyze that data to establish a protocol for procedures to follow.

One of the main mistakes schools make is to expect a software solution to fix all of their problems. Long before a search for hardware and software begins, educators should have extended discussions about their philosophy of education and how this philosophy will be enhanced by data warehousing software. Without an open forum and eventually large-scale agreements about the key elements of student learning, the software will merely be a container of numbers and the educators will be no better off (and possibly in a worse position because of the amount of energy needed to incorporate new strategies to please the software). Often hardware and software solutions are sold based on the skills of the marketing department and the sales force, rather than based on a philosophical fit with the educators in the school. Educators should closely examine their answers to the following questions:

- Do we have an agreed-on curriculum? The school should have specific details of what students should know and be able to do at each transition point (e.g., grade/course progression).
- Do we have an agreed-on method to qualitatively and quantitatively assess student learning?
- How will data be used? How will daily classroom interaction be affected by results?

What should I look for in an external vendor, and what makes a good fit?

As with any purchase, the term *caveat emptor* ("buyer beware") is appropriate here. This is not to imply that the companies who provide instructional/learning/data management systems are an unethical lot. Rather, most acquisitions that eventually fail do so because the decision-making educators have not clearly defined exactly what they want the software to do. The result is that schools end up spending large amounts of funds and training time on a solution that does not fit their needs.

All of the discussions contained in this chapter are needed to find the best fit with a vendor. Ultimately, schools must decide what it is they want the software solution to accomplish. That point can be truly arrived at only by using research paired with honest and comprehensive discussions to determine the current status of the district. Then, the educators charged with finding a "best fit" vendor can begin to narrow the field. Other key questions for educators to ponder might be:

- How well does the vendor know education and current educational issues?
- Are the trainers and technical support personnel well versed in educational topics?
- Does the vendor have a regional office and/or the ability to serve the school in a timely fashion?
- Is the hardware and software solution designed with modern and powerful specifications (e.g., is the solution designed with the latest industry standards)?
- What is the "total cost of ownership" of the solution? This could be based on:
  - initial software costs,
  - ongoing yearly update costs,
  - on-site training and support costs,
  - data migration costs,
  - required hardware costs,
  - required supplementary software costs, and
  - "ripple effect" costs (e.g., required costs associated with mandatory updates to server and workstations).

Best fit, like beauty, is in the eye of the beholder. It would be unwise for districts to assume that what worked for another district will automatically work equally as well for them. It takes a large number of vendors and solutions to meet the various needs of the educational community. It appears that many companies are designing powerfully robust solutions to assist educators with managing data in a meaningful way. The bottom line is to define exactly what is needed and clearly outline criteria to drive the purchase of the software solution. Once the solution is accomplished, then the educators in the district can go about the task of using authentic student learning data to drive the decision-making processes. The end result will be a better, more meaningful experience for each student.

Chapter 4

How to Understand Test Data

After accumulating data and using technology to break it down, the next step is to analyze the data in order to apply it to improve students' performance. For this purpose, data can be organized into three groupings: qualifying data, perceptions, and grades/test scores. Qualifying data can include demographic information, as well as rates for enrollment, attendance, disciplinary action, drop-outs, etc. Perceptions may include results from surveys and interviews, as well as formal and informal feedback.

This chapter focuses on test scores because they are often the most difficult to understand and analyze and because their analysis can lead to significant improvements on subsequent tests. Test scores require detailed analysis of student responses to the tests or assessments designed to parallel them and the provision of immediate and appropriate corrective instruction for individual students as indicated by that analysis.

Understanding Test Scores

Test scores can be presented in numerous ways. Understanding these scores is critical to understanding their relevancy.

Frequency distribution shows scores from highest to lowest (or vice versa) and how often each score occurs. For a grade level, for example, the frequency distribution might show that 50 students scored 89 on a criterion-referenced test, whereas only 15 students scored 95. Summarizing key data points into a simple layout, and the potentially necessary multiple measure systems required for it, may be daunting for school districts because of the large number of calculations that need to be done for every single student. Once an approach has been developed, however, all of the necessary calculations can be programmed into a computer system.

The key to presenting this data graphically is to put it into formats that can be quickly and easily understood. A format such as the one presented in Figure 4 offers readers an overview of information in a simple but effective presentation. The simplicity of the format avoids distortion of the numbers and encourages the reader to focus, not on the methodology or graphic design of the layout, but rather on the substance—in this case, students' results in attendance, language arts, and mathematics. Large sets of data (multiple test scores and grades and attendance data) are given coherence by providing one simple number—in the case of Figure 4, the number of students performing unsatisfactorily in a certain area. Color codes are used to highlight significant details, as in Figure 4 where red

Student Performance in Attendance, Language Arts, and Mathematics Second Quarter 2003, Grades 3-5								
Number of Students Performing Below Basic								
			Attendance		Language Arts		Math	
Teacher	Grade	Total Students	No.	Percent	No.	Percent	No.	Percent
Breeds	3	30	6	20%	5	17%	8	*27%*
Martinez	3	30	3	10%	8	*27%*	6	20%
Portner	3	28	4	14%	4	14%	6	21%
Layne	4	26	4	15%	8	*31%*	6	23%
Levinson	4	30	16	**53%**	16	**53%**	18	**60%**
McGee	4	28	18	**64%**	18	**64%**	14	**50%**
Cortez	5	31	4	13%	6	19%	10	*32%*
Mayfield	5	27	9	*33%*	4	15%	17	**63%**

Bold = More than half the class performed less than satisfactorily.
Bold Italic = Between one quarter and one half of the class performed less than satisfactorily.
For language, arts, and math, "unsatisfactory" means achieving a score of 75 percent or less.
Unsatisfactory attendance means missing more than 10 percent of school days in a quarter.

Figure 4 [23]

---

[23] With insight from Schmoker, Mike. *The Results Fieldbook: Practical Strategies from Dramatically Improved Schools*. Associations for Supervisions and Curriculum Development, 2001.

highlighting indicates that more than half the class is less than satisfactory. Patterns can be easily seen in this type of format—for example, two of the fourth grade classrooms with a significant number of students performing less than satisfactorily in math and language arts also have significant attendance problems.

Descriptive statistics are another effective means of summarizing and describing a set of scores accurately. One set of descriptive statistics is measures of position, including rank and percentile rank. Another set, measures of central tendency, includes mean, median, and mode. A third set—range, standard deviation, and probable error—indicates measures of variability.

Different scales are used to express students' performances on tests. A student's raw score is the number of correct responses to the test questions (for example 84). Although this score provides the information that the student correctly answered 84 (out of, say, a possible 90) questions, more information may be determined about the student's performance by looking at additional data. For example, the student's performance may be viewed differently depending on whether the mean (average) score on the test was 64 or 80.

Percentages are a common way of expressing test scores results, with 100 percent indicating a perfect score, and 0 percent indicating the absolute lower limit. Percentages are useful for indicating performance, but they should be avoided in some situations. For example, the raw scores of very short tests should not be transformed into percentages because one raw score point difference could become a large increment as a percentage. For example, missing one question on a five-question test would result in a score of only 80 percent.

Percentiles are another way of expressing test score results, specifically on a normed test. They are the scale most frequently used in reporting standardized test results, and they are used to compare a student's place within a relative population, so they are considered normative. In a percentile scale, the population of students taking a test is divided into 100. The lowest-scoring one-hundredth receives a raw score within a range at the lowest end, and so on for successive hundredths. A percentile rank is a student's relative position within a specified group. For example, a student who received a raw score of 86/90 might rate in the 98th percentile on a certain test. This means the student would have received a raw score higher than 97 percent of his or her peers taking the test. Percentiles can also be expressed as a decile, or any one of nine points separating the frequency into ten groups of equal size.

It is important to note that percentiles should never be added, subtracted, or averaged because the distance between points is not equal. The points are farther apart at the upper and lower ends of the scale than in the middle because the majority of scores are found to be in the middle.

Standard age scores are another type of normalized score. These scores can be used when a variable is influenced by age. The effect age plays on scores can be found by organizing the scores from different age-groups as separate distributions. Grade equivalent scores express performance in terms of the grade and month at which a particular score represents typical performance. A grade level score indicates that the student's score is equal to the group average of students in that grade. It is often suggested that educators avoid the use of grade- and age-equivalent scoring because it is easily misinterpreted.

The **normal probability curve** (Figure 5), also called a bell curve, is used to indicate what often happens in test scores when they are given to large numbers of people. With the normal curve, the

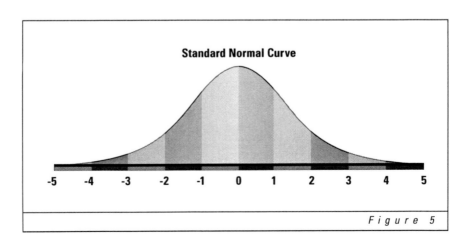

Standard Normal Curve

-5 -4 -3 -2 -1 0 1 2 3 4 5

Figure 5

majority of students receive a score somewhere close to the mean. The fewest number of scores are received at the ends of the scale. The left and right halves of the curve are mirror images of each other.

With **standardized scores**, there is an equal standard deviation on each side of a mean score. The standard deviation is calculated by squaring each student's difference from the mean, adding the sum of these squares, averaging the squares' total, and then finding the square root of the average[24]. Data from a group of students is used to calculate deviation units. For example, in the case where the mean raw score on a test is 72 and the standard deviation is 4.6, a score of 77 (72.4 + 4.6) would have a deviation score of +0.4. The units of deviation are rarely greater than 5. Negative values can be eliminated on a five point deviation scale by adding 5 to every deviation unit. This changes the mean from 0 to 5, making the lowest value 0 and the highest value 10.

Standardized scores can be further transformed to a one hundred point scale by multiplying by 10. The mean would become 50 (5 x 10), with a standard deviation of 10 (1 x 10).

Stanines and **stens** are divisions of the standardized normal scale that can be used to indicate approximately where a student's test scores fall within a population. Stanines are based on a standard score of nine units (1 through 9). Unlike other standard scores, which have a specific value, stanines represent bands of values. Each stanine, except for 1 and 9, is equal to one-half of a standard deviation in width. The mean is the midpoint of the middle stanine, which is 5 (Figure 6, page 62).

Stens are normalized standard scores with ten units (1 through 10). The score 5.5 is considered the mean, and there are five normalized standard score units on each side of the mean. As with stanines, each of the stens is equal to one-half of a standard deviation unit, except for the values of 1 and 10, which are open-ended (Figure 7, page 62).

---

[24] McCallum, Ian and Ray Sumner. *Using Data for Monitoring and Target Setting.* Routledge, 1999.

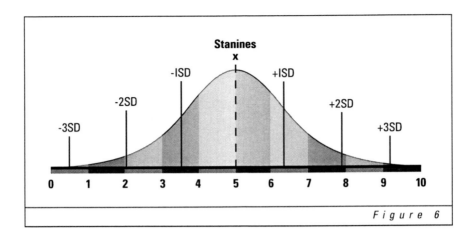

Figure 6

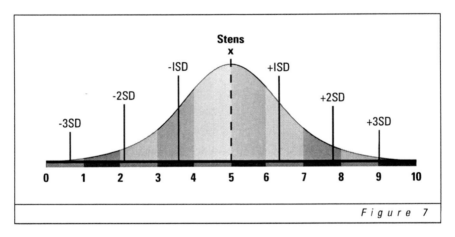

Figure 7

Looking for Trends

Once data has been broken down and presented in an easily understood manner, the next step is to look for trends within the data. Educators might ask the following questions:

- What are student's successes/weaknesses?
- Which students barely passed?
- What concepts are most students learning or missing?
- What concepts are high-level students not understanding?
- What concepts are low-performing students understanding?
- What are patterns across grade levels and within content areas?
- What are demographic distinctions?

- What sustained mastery or weaknesses are there at the individual, classroom, subgroups, grade, campus, and district levels[25]?

In attempting to look for trends, educators are often discouraged by the different types of tests and standards developed by the state from year to year. However, these variations should not be viewed as a roadblock. When switching types of tests, states may provide correlation-prediction factors that can help educators determine how their current results will align with previous results. What is important is to focus on what was tested and to find parallels in content matter. This may involve creating a template to standardize how results on specific topics are presented. In Figure 8 (page 64) for example, students are broken into five groups—advanced, proficient, basic, below basic, and remedial—based on their test results in four language arts areas. Students can be placed into these groupings no matter what the type of test given, based on the categories of reading fiction, reading nonfiction, composition, and grammar. In Figure 8, grammar, usage, and mechanics is shown to be an area requiring re-teaching for some students, with 11 percent of students testing at the remedial level for this skill set.

This approach can help in other apples-to-oranges comparisons—such as when comparing performance on a reading assessment, end-of-unit multiple-choice test, and oral presentation—by comparing data points and student mastery on the subject addressed through each test.

As detailed in Chapter 2, the process of breaking down data begins with simple numbers, such as breaking down numbers by race, gender, or eligibility for free or reduced lunches. The next step is to determine how this data has changed over time (i.e., to view changes in categorical variables). Educators will then look at how specific categorical variables correlate with others (e.g., they might look at the number of students in the lowest-performing quartile and how many attended the district's pre-kindergarten program).

---

[25] Barksdale, Mary. *8 Steps to Student Success.* Equity in Education, 2003.

The final step in the process is to answer more complex questions about students' performance. Such questions might include: What teachers have best practices to share with other teachers? What teachers need immediate assistance? How quickly do students new to the district reach standards? Does a higher level of attendance correlate to higher standardized test scores, and vice versa?

When looking for trends, it is important for educators to first look over the data and develop a first impression. When doing so, educators should consider whether their performance results match

Language Arts Assessment - Sunnydale District (Percentage of Students by Achievement Level)				
Achievement Level	Reading Fiction (1,500 students assessed)	Reading Nonfiction (1,500 students assessed)	Composition (1,500 students assessed)	Grammar, Usage, and Mechanics (1,500 students assessed)
Advanced	8%	6%	4%	3%
Proficient	38%	42%	36%	36%
Basic	40%	36%	37%	32%
Below Basic	7%	10%	16%	18%
Remedial	7%	6%	7%	11%

Figure 8

expectations set by the district and the state and whether their overall results seem high or low. Educators might also consider comparing their results to those in another district (or if it seems pertinent, to results for the entire state). This will help them get an idea of where their students stand in relation to others.

Once educators have a first impression of results, they can then examine the data in further detail by looking at the spread or distribution of the data. Doing so provides further analysis of a school's performance because it helps educators pinpoint specific strengths and weaknesses. Knowing where strengths and weaknesses lie is critical for educators when they develop an instructional curriculum.

Translating the data into concrete terms is the next step in the process of looking for trends. To simplify the process and help people remember the data, it is often helpful to use one set of statistics to represent a large set of data. This set can easily be compared to other values, such as results at other schools. However, because this single statistic does not provide educators with everything they need to know about their students, it is important to present a description of the spread of data along with the single set of statistics. When measuring the spread, you may want to list the range of the data, identify outliers, or separate the data into quartiles or deciles.

Data relating to the achievement of subpopulations can provide important information for a school district. When comparing and contrasting subpopulations, educators should look for significant trends in the data and evaluate trends and differences. They should look at the inputs, processes, and outputs (see page 28 for a description of these terms) that may be coming into play in differences among subgroups[26]. When looking at the relationships among the input, process, and outputs, educators should look for positive correlations, negative correlations, or no correlations. With positive correlations, two indicators would move in the same direction, for example, increased study time might correlate with increased test scores. With negative correlations, two indicators would move in the opposite direction, for example, a decrease in parental involvement might correlate with an increase in attendance problems. No correlation would indicate that two events appear to be unaffected by each other; for example, a donation from a local business might have no effect on a student's test scores. Educators might test their assumption about relationships among related outcomes, practices, and inputs by graphing data for two indicators, such as test-preparation time and test scores, looking for clear upward or downward trends that would support assumptions[27].

---

[26] Bradby, Denise, Karen Levesque, Kristi Rossi, and Peter Teitelbaum. *At Your Fingertips: Using Everyday Data to Improve Schools.* MPR Associates Inc., 1998.
[27] Bradby, Denise, Karen Levesque, Kristi Rossi, and Peter Teitelbaum. *At Your Fingertips: Using Everyday Data to Improve Schools.* MPR Associates Inc., 1998.

However, educators should remember that two events occurring at the same time does not necessarily indicate a cause-and-effect relationship. In fact, many additional factors may be at work. For example, it might appear that a group of students performed particularly poorly during the second quarter as a result of a significant change in the curriculum. However, further investigation may show that low attendance rates due to a flu bug during the quarter were a significant factor in the low performance. In such a case, it would be important for educators to closely monitor the next quarter's results.

Chapter 5

How Data Can Be Used at Each Level

Often, education lacks the quality assurance we see in business, government, and health care. Instead of other forms of quality assurance offered to businesses, educators use tests. Because of a demanding schedule, they teach, test, score, and then record the score in a grade book. After that, it is on to the next lesson or grade level. Often in the past, tests have tended to be used to end an instructional activity rather than to start the next activity. In other words, test results have documented success—or failure—in the previous process rather than facilitating success in preparing for the next process. With few exceptions, both the successful and the unsuccessful student were sent on to the next phase.

Obviously, test scores should not languish in some file. Data itself is impotent and becomes useful only as a tool to facilitate improvements in results. Once educators have learned how to properly understand data, they can use test results—and other data—to help students achieve and exceed standards by adjusting teaching approaches, the classroom experience, and the campus environment based on student needs.

How Data Can Help

The most important aspect of data disaggregation is applying data at each level. After all, disaggregating data is simply a means to improving the quality of education for every student. At the classroom, campus, district, regional, and/or state levels, data can help to[28]:

- measure student achievement;

[28] Bernhardt, Victoria L. *Data Analysis for Comprehensive Schoolwide Improvement.* Eye on Education Inc., 1998.
Barksdale, Mary L, with Patricia W. Davenport. *An Educator's Guide to Implementing Continuous Improvement*, 2003.

- identify students who are falling behind;
- highlight effective and/or ineffective teaching approaches and processes and instructional content;
- guide students and provide information to parents;
- report for the NCLB act and state requirements;
- help find the root causes of problems;
- identify where to allocate resources;
- focus on goals and gauge performance against those goals;
- reveal trends, changes, and what to prepare for;
- assess needs for mission-critical issues;
- confirm/reject assumptions and have a common understanding for discussions; and
- promote accountability.

The bottom line is that data is a necessary tool for continuous improvement. Data reveals what needs to be improved and what is working to do so. It also helps to align perceptions and assumptions with reality. This applies to student achievement, curriculum, problem areas, and performance issues for entire schools and smaller groupings of students. Let's now dig deeper to look at how data can support some of the primary roles in improving student performance.

- **Parents**—With results such as those reported through the NCLB act, parents will be aware of their child's strengths and weaknesses and how well schools are performing. The federal government reports that parents will have other options and resources for helping their children if their schools are chronically in need of improvement. Additional information throughout the year can help parents reinforce lessons in the classroom and highlight where special attention is needed.
- **Teachers**—Teachers have powerful control over how data will be recognized and leveraged. By embracing relevant and valid data, teachers can objectively evaluate each student's subject mastery and the approaches most effective for teaching. As a consequence, teachers can adjust lesson plans and individualize approaches where possible and where needed. Students can also be grouped by test results or study methods to proceed. The

Author's perspective:
Randy McDaniel discusses exposure to data.

Most schools have a large number of educational professionals. Not all of these are traditional classroom teachers. Many are special education teachers, Title 1 teachers, speech therapists, curriculum experts, and building level and central office level administrators. Additionally, other licensed and/or support personnel, such as tutors and summer school instructors, exist. We contend that every educator in the school should be in tune with the child's learning data. Each educator, regardless of whether he or she is a special education teacher or an after-school tutoring coordinator, should have access to and a deep understanding of the learning data of the children being served.

It should go without argument that each learning activity sponsored by the school should specifically address the needs of each child. No child should be exposed to group learning activities that do not address his or her needs and/or serve as a precursor to future opportunities.

federal government reports that, because of the NCLB act, teachers will have the training and resources they need for teaching effectively, using curriculum that is grounded in scientifically based research.

- **School psychologists**—School psychologists often have excellent training in interpreting and analyzing test results. Consequently, they are in a position to help both teachers and administrators understand raw data and test results, as well as work directly with students to identify any challenges they may be facing.

- **Principals**—Principals are typically expected to use data in determining the school's progress by distinctions such as classroom, subject, and grade. As well as providing direction for the overall school, principals can redirect time and resources to problem areas. In addition, with the NCLB act, the federal government states that principals will have information they need to strengthen their schools' weaknesses and to put into practice methods and strategies backed by sound, scientific research.

- **Superintendents**—Superintendents set the tone for the district in leveraging data to make informed decisions. In addition to generally assessing each campus, the superintendent can create a safe environment for data-driven decision making[29]. Superintendents must encourage staff to systematically apply data and, accordingly, should arrange for training for staff members to understand results. Along with principals, superintendents should take charge in assessing what data is available, what can be compiled for a comprehensive picture, and what should be leveraged in decision making. Again, because of the NCLB act, the federal government assures educators that superintendents will be able to measure how their districts are doing and compare their districts to others across the state. In doing so, they will have more and better information on which to based decisions about priorities in their districts.
- **All administrators**—Leaders guide through guarantees, actions, and routines. Data allows all administrators to make informed decisions and address larger issues affecting students. It also allows administrators to interact with the community, bolstered by objective information.

All administrators have specific responsibilities to teachers as well. The NCLB act does not recognize all the teachers who invest time and effort to help a student dramatically improve, even though he/she still might not pass. Therefore, it is the administrator's responsibility to reward and encourage these teachers for contributing to a student's future accomplishments. After all, even though a dramatically improving child may not pass a state test this year, his or her progress will make passing next year's test more attainable.

The ability to make informed decisions is bolstered by standardized test results and other data throughout the educational system, from regional and state administrators to governors, community leaders, and volunteer groups. An important issue is

---

[29] American Association of School Administrators. *Using Data to Improve Schools.* 2002

how all of these roles work together in leveraging data. The key is not each level using data separately, but superintendents working side-by-side with other administrators, teachers, principals, and parents. Everyone strives toward a common goal, and there is the possibility for meaningful, ongoing dialogue among education stakeholders by focusing discussions and decisions on facts and not opinion.

This kind of setting requires an atmosphere of trust. Teachers must trust that administrators will not punish them when results are lower than expected, and administrators must empower teachers to leverage data in the classroom so that instruction can be customized as needed for students to reach goals. Business leader W. Edwards Deming once admonished leaders to "drive out fear." In education at present, driving out fear is critical because accountability and assessments are increasingly at the forefront in determining what makes a successful school. If fear is prevalent throughout a school, then there will be many roadblocks as educators wrestle with how best to address any areas of deficiencies.

In *Data Analysis for Comprehensive Schoolwide Improvement* (Eye on Education Inc., 1998), Victoria L. Bernhardt advised that:

> *Teachers will be more inclined to change the way they do business when they are part of identifying the problems and the solutions. Look at the results of each of the analyses included in the larger comprehensive analysis. Use all the data together to predict what needs to be done differently to get different results.*

However, for everyone to work together, certain misperceptions will need to be overcome. The first misperception is that all students cannot be expected to meet certain standards. Marked as "the soft bigotry of low expectations" by President Bush, this is a notion frequently discounted. Race, socioeconomic status, and gender do not determine a student's capabilities and are never a valid excuse.

Even when educators value leveraging data in decision making, there may be a misperception that doing so is not their job. APQC has found that the more thoroughly people are trained in a subject, the more likely they are to understand that they have a responsibility to address it. The NCLB act has somewhat clarified this expectation, but it is up to districts and schools to ensure that all educators understands their role in maintaining data sources and leveraging that data.

To overcome transitional challenges, it is advisable to make data reporting a frequent, commonplace event. This eliminates surprise test results and provides more detailed feedback on student progress. Overall, it is important not to dump piles of data on educators. Data must be filtered for validity and relevancy.

Focus on Informed Acts of Improvement

After laying the groundwork by determining what data matters most, finding implications in it, and aligning it with goals, stakeholders are ready to use the data to develop a plan to alter processes, practices, and approaches. This plan will likely involve changing classroom processes, adjusting the curriculum, or addressing individual issues.

The challenges to altering classroom processes, the curriculum, or individual student performance based on test scores and other data throughout the year is obvious: teachers have a lot to cover, and there is an assumption that regularly adjusting plans makes it more likely that the class won't cover mandated curriculum by the end of the year. This assumption is exactly what the NCLB act attempts to counter. "Sticking to the plan," regardless of the performance of each student, adds to the problem; it leaves some students behind and compounds their academic challenges as they are forced to proceed as if they understand everything that has already been covered.

The NCLB act does not identify specific steps for determining how data can bolster each goal; in this most important stage, it is up to educators to apply their knowledge, experience, and creativity to develop solutions. This determination will be affected by how current results compare to goals. For example, if students are not passing standardized tests, despite that being the goal, educators should look at how far away they are from reaching the goal. They should also ask: What data will help students and teachers assess problematic areas before students take the test? And how can that data be leveraged to improve individual student achievement—and

Author's perspective:
Paige Leavitt discusses how to implement an improvement initiative.
   With every effort to alter processes, practices, and approaches, stakeholders will need to develop an implementation plan. To get started, stakeholders should take into account their current status relative to their goals. They should develop a clear, tangible picture for staff and teachers of the initiative as it relates to the identified goals. Simple definitions and language should be used to introduce the change, as well as to explain how data was leveraged to make this decision. Stakeholders should identify which educators will be affected and how to get their support. As with any improvement initiative, stakeholders must take into consideration the campus/district culture and previous barriers to achieving the goal. Data can be used as evidence of how the initiative will ultimately improve students' performance.

   In the next step of the implementation plan, a strategy should be developed. Who will facilitate the plan? That is, who will ensure the plan is implemented, and who will enforce new standards based on the initiative? Will this require additional resources and from where? Stakeholders should communicate and market this strategy.

   A critical step in the implementation of an improvement initiative is, obviously, to launch the change. With an adequate strategy, this point will involve simply carrying out the strategy, including funding the change and assessing what was learned during the implementation. Adjustments can be expected, but responsibility for monitoring implementation and making adjustments should be spelled out in the plan.

   The final step is to institutionalize the change. Ensure it becomes a part of the "way we work," and monitor adherence. As educators become comfortable with leveraging data in decision making, it is important for the stakeholders to detail the changed processes and approaches. This will ensure that the same data is used from year to year and that results are documented in the same way as time progresses.

   Critical success factors in leveraging data to improve include: maintaining committed and involved stakeholders to ensure data is leveraged to reach goals and make improvements; having a consistent vision of how data will be leveraged and what goals it will support; initiating change when and where people are ready; and communicating constantly and effectively about data and the inferences made from it.

consequently, test scores? It will also be helpful to look at data concerning what instructional approaches are effective, what students feel is challenging and helpful, how the population's and students' needs are shifting, what items students received low scores on in previous years, and training that staff and teachers have received in interpreting test results and other data.

The NCLB act proceeds under the premise that educators will direct students having trouble with certain areas to those instructional methods that will yield the fastest, most dramatic improvements. Any leveraging of instruction-focused data to improve decision making—and ultimately, student performance—will likely indicate that different students require different processes, practices, and approaches. Consequently, the stakeholders involved in selecting data to focus on should prepare teachers and staff for the likelihood that additional time and instruction for certain students will be needed. Individual student attention is a necessity in improving overall student performance.

As this section indicates, data disaggregation is merely the first step in the larger continuous improvement journey mandated by the NCLB act. This section has summarized how this data can be acted on, and APQC has a number of publications listed in the back of this book for more detailed information on various continuous improvement approaches. One of the most successful, but also most simple, approaches to using data as a kick start to significant improvement is the eight-step process first developed in Brazosport, Texas. This process is introduced in the following section in order to illustrate how disaggregated data can be used[30].

An Exceptional Example: The Eight-step Instructional Process

Data disaggregation is the first step in the eight-step instructional process, a continuous improvement teaching and learning cycle that has been proven to help students succeed.

---

[30] *Closing the Achievement Gap: No Excuses* (2001) and *Educators in Action: Examining Successful Improvement Efforts* (2004), both published by APQC, provide examples of how the eight-step process has been applied in real school districts across the nation.

The eight-step process is based on the Plan/Do/Check/Act approach: 1) make a plan spurred by valid and relevant data (plan); 2) teach on the basis of that plan (do); 3) assess the results of that instruction (check); and 4) make adjustments to instructional practices based on follow-up data to then get even better results (act). Faculty experience is the foundation of the process.

The eight-step process involves the following steps:

1. disaggregate data,
2. develop an instructional timeline,
3. deliver the instructional focus,
4. administer frequent assessments,
5. use tutorials to re-teach,
6. provide enrichment opportunities,
7. reinforce lessons, and
8. monitor progress.

Step 1, data disaggregation, involves acknowledging that instructional improvement begins with recognizing how things really are; data indicates where students are relative to where they should be. Educators should examine the strengths and weaknesses revealed by numbers and then plan improvements. They should establish crucial priorities by manually ranking the skills sets from weakest to strongest. Data disaggregation can be used to identify instructional groups within the classroom, such as students needing re-teaching and students who have mastered the skills taught. This book is your guide to Step 1.

Teachers can summarize and examine the strengths and weaknesses of their students using a profile like the one in Figure 9 (page 76).

Step 2, developing an instructional timeline, involves creating a schedule for instruction and assessment. Educators should begin with areas that the analysis of disaggregated data indicate hold the greatest opportunities for improvement. They should determine what specific areas have the greatest number of students that need help and which standards have the greatest weight on the assessment. This can reveal what teachers should be emphasizing in the instruction (and beget an efficient approach that might allow for

Language Arts Assessment Profile	1. Sue	2. Robin	3. Kris	4. Ramon	5. Victor	6. Rick
Teacher: _____ Class: _____						
Language Arts Objective 1 Fiction						
Identify main idea.						
Identify cause-and-effect relationships.						
Identify author's purpose.						
Summarize the main points.						
Language Arts Objective 2 Nonfiction						
Identify theme.						
Analyze the effect of setting on plot.						
Identify the main conflict.						
Identify the climax.						
Identify the genre.						
Evaluate literary merit.						

Figure 9

additional time that can be redirected at students having trouble and at problematic topics). And anything worth emphasizing in the instruction is worth gauging through regular assessment.

In schools with an instructional timeline, students within a grade level work on the same skills at the same time. This gives teachers of all subjects the opportunity to work together as a team to achieve a common goal. Teachers can collaborate by sharing insights on challenges and best instructional practices, and they can work with students to explain how a week's skill relates to different subjects. For example, if a curriculum calendar indicates that students in Grade 9 will focus on cause and effect this week, then this skill can be integrated into every class. For example, a language arts teacher might have students look for causes and effects in a short

Achieving Mastery of State Standards

For students to achieve mastery of state standards, it is critical that budget allocations, teacher training, and staff evaluations be tied to content standards[31]. Schools must allocate funds for the purchase of equipment, such as computer programs, to meet content standards. Teacher training must also be tied to standards—teachers must have the expertise required to tie current lesson plans to what students have already learned and what they'll need to be taught in the future. In addition, teacher and administrator evaluations should be closely tied to students' success in learning state standards. School-site plans, documents that elaborate on teacher training in standards, student report cards, teacher grade books, and evaluations can all be used to determine how closely standards are being followed.

Every teacher in the district should be provided with an opportunity to review results. Achieving mastery of standards cannot occur without this step. Review involves focusing on improvement and resource issues. Questions to ask during review include the following:

- Are teachers experts in the subject-areas they are teaching? If not, what training do they need?
- Have teachers been given the opportunity to observe successful experienced colleagues?
- Are teachers being encouraged to benefit from their peers' expertise and experience by using them for help while developing their lesson plans?
- Who is responsible for making sure that instructional improvement strategies used in the classroom are most effective?
- Are teachers being given sufficient time to meet and collaborate with their peers?
- Are teachers working in teams to ensure their lessons are most effective?
- Are lesson plans specifically designed to address skills students need to learn and to re-teach skills students require extra help on?
- Do teachers know how many of their students are succeeding on key performance tests?
- Do teachers know if students' scores are improving during the year and from year to year?
- Do teachers know what areas of performance students are strong or weak in?

---

[31] Ardovino, Joan, John Hollingsworth, and Silvia Ybarra. *Multiple Measures: Accurate Ways to Assess Student Achievement.* Corwin Press, Inc., 2000.

story, a science teacher might have students compose a cause-and-effect chain for environmental pollution, and a social studies teacher might have students determine the causes and effects of World War II. The development of timelines lets everyone work on a common plan and also allows for skills to be taught in an appropriate sequence—from simple to complex.

A key aspect of this step is for teachers to work with students to set focused and tangible challenges based directly on their past performance and their explicit goals. By identifying proven practices through data, teachers can set realistic but challenging goals for each individual student to meet. Just like the curriculum, these student goals are aligned with campus and district goals and state standards. Because of the systems the central office has put in place, teachers are in the best position to set these goals and make them explicit to students. These goals should be manageable, measurable, and focused. For example, a goal to improve third grade proficiency levels on the math portion of a state assessment by 10 percent from last year's results would then translate into identifying what help each third grader needs to reach proficiency. For each student, instruction is provided on the knowledge gaps, along with a clear understanding for the student of what he or she needs to work on. (Such small, incremental, and measurable goals will help the campus and district to achieve established, long-term goals.)

Having analyzed data, listed priorities and goals, and established an instructional schedule, the next step, Step 3, involves teachers actually delivering the instructional focus—the lessons and resources that have been planned so carefully in Step 2. In this step, teachers use the needs of their students as a guide to design unique and appropriate lesson plans to teach the required skills. Teachers develop lesson plans and engage students in learning. Although the instructional calendar specifies what should be focused on, it is up to the teachers to design appropriate lesson plans based on individual data results. This step also involves support from all other educators in reinforcing the learning objectives designated on the instructional calendar.

The continuous assessment of Step 4 should ideally involve all students taking formal assessments throughout the year. The tests should be given frequently to allow teachers to make adjustments to instruction based on students' achievements. It would be understandable for teachers to be overwhelmed at the idea of developing comprehensive assessments every few weeks. Short, multiple-choice quizzes on the skill being taught may suffice when time and money prevent other options. (To combat time constraints, some school districts are using Web-based assessment developers to provide tests and analysis of test-result data within days of testing.) Teachers can keep track of students' achievement on these tests by using a standards-based grade book (Figure 10). These books highlight areas of needed improvement by showing how students perform on each objective. In addition to letting teachers know where students need extra help, frequent testing also gives teachers instant feedback on the effectiveness of certain teaching methods. It also allows teachers to know immediately which students are mastering content and which need further assistance. With this testing, students, teachers, and parents in a school district should be assured that students are well-prepared for state assessments.

Assessment Chart						
Name	Scale	Score	Standard 1.a Context Clues	Standard 1.b Suffixes	Standard 1.c Prefixes	Standard 1.d Latin roots
Allen, Charlie	A	75	18	19	18	20
Bjorn, Karen	C	63	15	16	14	18
Edward, Bob	B	69	17	18	17	17
Fanon, Mark	A	79	19	20	20	20
Gonzales, Ed	A	77	18	19	20	20
Jack, Marie	C-	57	19	10	14	14
Kenny, Juan	B+	70	18	17	16	19
Layne, Sophie	B	69	17	18	16	18
Little, Maggie	A	80	20	20	20	20
Mack, Jason	D+	55	14	14	14	13

Figure 10

In Step 5, groups of teachers use the data they gathered in Step 4 to either continue with the instructional timeline they've developed or to modify the schedule to accommodate students' having difficulty. This step involves frequent tutoring for those students having trouble so that they can stay on track with the curriculum calendar. Designed to ensure no child is left behind, Step 5 gives teachers the option to try a new teaching method or to give individual or small group instruction to students who have yet to master a skill.

In turn, Step 6 involves providing enrichment for those that succeed. Teachers should make enrichment activities enticing so that all students will want to participate in them. Step 6 ensures that high-achieving students can learn new material and master more-complex skills while their lower-achieving peers are provided with re-teaching.

In Step 7, teachers provide frequent maintenance to ensure that students retain what they have learned. This step acknowledges the fact that mastery of skills does not occur overnight and that students may need to be exposed to a subject several times before they achieve mastery. Frequent reviews should be a part of the instructional timeline for every school wanting students to master standards.

Step 8 requires that a team of colleagues, including superintendents and principals frequently attend classrooms to monitor instruction. Rather than being a "punitive process," this step is designed to ensure that all teachers and students are working successfully toward a common goal: academic excellence. Superintendents and principals can show that they are committed to the process and can therefore encourage teachers to succeed. In addition, they can keep track of best practices they witness in individual classrooms and share these practices with other teachers.

The ultimate goal of the eight-step process is that all decisions regarding student instruction be data-driven. Once educators see the value of using data to drive instruction, they will likely be disinclined to use instructional methods not based on data

This is "a gradual process of proof." Success in data disaggregation is deemed by four regularly occurring actions[32]:

1. using a variety of data effectively;
2. using information to improve instructional practice;
3. using data to affect student performance; and
4. aligning investments, outcomes, and improvement strategies.

By using the eight-step process, you can ensure that your data disaggregation efforts will transform into an ongoing performance indicator system. The key is to collect data on an ongoing basis, interpret trends, and sustain or modify improvement efforts. This is the foundation for systematic improvement that leaves no student behind.

Author's perspective:
Randy McDaniel discusses the challenges of teaching against the clock.

Much has been written about the time-based nature of education. Bells, buses, and schedules drive the day, courses, semesters, years, and ultimately the amount of time devoted to student learning. Therefore, time—not learning—is the constant in American education, and learning is the variable. The rule is simple: learn what you can in the time made available. It should surprise no one that some bright, hard-working students do reasonably well. Other students, from the typical student to the dropout, often run into trouble[33]. The boundaries of student growth are defined by schedules for bells, buses, and vacations instead of standards for students and learning.

If experience, research, and common sense teach nothing else, they confirm the truism that people learn at different rates and in different ways with different subjects.

Educators often criticize the amount of time devoted to learning with the statement, "There's isn't enough time to get everything required into the day." If this is true, then how can data help?

---

[32] American Association of School Administrators. *Using Data to Improve Schools.*
[33] National Education Commission on Time and Learning. "Prisoners of Time." Washington, D.C., 1994.

A review of the loss of instructional and learning time is needed to fully understand the impact of time and learning. One of the largest "thieves" of time lost in American education today is the yearly event of reviewing to start the school year. For many classrooms, a review of content may last four to eight weeks at the start of every year. The amount of instruction and learning time devoted to this practice is staggering. The practice of reviewing previously learned material to build on that knowledge and move forward in a meaningful way is not inherently wrong; on the contrary, it is educationally sound. What is wrong is the assumption that every student in each classroom needs exactly the same amount of review—and review on the same material. The challenge for educators is to tailor instruction each day to maximize academic learning time. We believe the only way this can occur is to have accurate and timely student learning data, which then drives the design of instruction.

A much superior method of starting the school year would be to make sure each educator received accurate and specific academic data on each student in the class as early in the summer as possible (or before the course began in classes that do not start in the fall). With this knowledge, educators could make review a meaningful experience. For example, a second grade teacher might find out that 7 of her 24 students have not yet mastered a key mathematical concept. This then would naturally lead to her forming groups to address this concept (either in a cooperative learning cross-grouping technique or in learning pods pairing students with similar learning skills). This would allow these students to catch up while other students learn new or more advanced skills. The groundwork that must be laid to accomplish the aforementioned scenario is relatively straightforward:

- Make sure the school's adopted curriculum is well known and taught by each educator.
- Make sure that quality instructional resources are available to each educator and that each educator has the training necessary to implement the curriculum.
- Make sure each grade/course in the school's curriculum is aligned to ensure the maximum amount of integration and eliminate as much gap and overlap as possible.
- Provide educators with diagnostic assessments and reporting methodologies that are well understood and used throughout the school.

A similar loss of individual instructional time exists throughout the school year. Given the fact that students learn at different rates, the practice of whole group instruction for a majority of lessons and having all students working on the same lesson for the same amount of time appear inefficient. For example, students that have mastered the key curriculum elements of a lesson on day three of a five-day unit typically must wait while the final two days of instruction are completed. At the other end of the scale the student who has yet to master the key curriculum elements will be asked to move forward with the entire group at the end of the fifth day, ready or not. It appears that attempting to use whole group instruction throughout the K-12 system will result in two outcomes: some students will indeed be left behind and high-performing students will not achieve all they possibly can.

Another key element to the amount of instructional time is the curriculum itself. Educators at all levels must make difficult decisions regarding curriculum.

- Is the K-12 curriculum tightly aligned from grade level to grade level?
- Does are curriculum focus on minor points of the curriculum at the detriment of the major curriculum items?
- Has the teaching staff mapped the curriculum to the school calendar to ensure that the written curriculum can actually fit within the given instructional time?
- Does the curriculum spend major time on minor curriculum items?

Education stakeholders can make a significant impact in the time vs. learning struggle with honest evaluations of questions such as these.

Appendix

Technology Support Index

Domain One - Equipment Standards

	Emergent	Islands	Integrated	Exemplary	Fiscal
Cycling of Equipment	No replacement cycle has been defined.	Equipment is placed on a replacement cycle greater than 5 years.	Equipment is placed on a 4–5-year replacement cycle.	Equipment is placed on a 3-year replacement cycle.	$$$$
Brand Selection (e.g., Compaq, Dell, Apple, IBM, etc.)	No brands are specified, purchasing is done by price only, and is site controlled.	A district brand is selected, but changes from year to year depending upon what vendor is providing the best selection at the time.	A district brand has been selected, but isn't strictly enforced allowing for purchase of some equipment that is outside the standard.	A district brand has been specified, and all purchases are made within that brand over an extended period of time.	Neutral
Model Selection	There are no limitations on model selection.	A model line has been selected, but many choices are given within that line.	A model line has been selected, and choices are limited to 3–5 models.	Model selection is limited to one or two, with few variations.	Neutral
Platform (e.g., Apple, Windows, Sun)	The district supports two or more platforms, and platform choice is left to individuals in the district.	The district supports two or more platforms, but choices are made by schools at large and are generally uniform.	The district supports two platforms, but choices are limited to program areas.	One platform is selected for the district, with few exceptions for special projects.	Neutral
Standard Operating System (OS) (e.g., Win 3.x, Win95, Win98, Win2K, Mac 8, Mac 9, Apple II, etc.)	Four or more OS versions are used, and all are " supported" by the district.	Three OS versions are used, and the older OS computers are migrated or aren't supported.	Two OS versions are used, with most equipment migrated to the most recent OS.	One OS version is used district-wide, with all computers migrated to that OS.	$$
Application Software Standard	No software standards have been established.	Software standards are established. Nonstandard installations are permitted and some support is provided.	Software standards are established. Nonstandard installations are allowed but no support is provided.	Software standards are established and only those applications on the list are permitted on computers.	Neutral
Donated Equipment	Donated equipment is accepted with no regard to whether it meets district equipment standards.	Donated equipment is accepted with minimum performance requirements with no regard to brand or age.	Donated equipment is accepted with minimum performance requirements and suggested brand. Equipment is less than 3 years old.	Donated equipment is accepted but only if it meets specific brand, model, performance, and system requirements. Equipment is less than 2 years old. Cash donations are encouraged so new equipment can be purchased.	Neutral
Granted Equipment	Grant equipment decisions are made by the grantee or grantor and aren't influenced by the district.	The district is consulted regarding grant equipment. Cash grant equipment is purchased according to the standard. Equipment grants are readily accepted regardless of brand.	All cash grants meet district specifications. Equipment grants are approved before submittal, by the technology department. Standardization is encouraged.	All grant equipment, purchased and given, must meet district specification or it isn't allowed on the district network or in the school.	Neutral

Developed by Dr. Chip Kimball (ckimball@iste.org) in conjunction with ISTE and the Gates Foundation.

iste

Version 1.10

Technology Support Index

Domain One - Equipment Standards

	Emergent	Islands	Integrated	Exemplary	Fiscal
Peripheral Standards (e.g., printers, scanners, digital cameras, projectors, video, etc.)	No peripheral standards are set.	Peripherals are standardized by brand but models within the brand aren't. The peripheral standards change frequently and are rated for consumer use.	Peripherals are standardized by brand and model, but the list contains many options with many consumer-rated items.	All peripherals are standardized, with specific models identified that are primarily rated for enterprise use. Brands and models are limited.	$
Surplus practice	Equipment isn't added to surplus until it is no longer usable and is supported as resources allow.	Surplus equipment is supported by district personnel but as a low priority.	Surplus equipment is no longer supported by district personnel but can be used by schools until it breaks.	Surplus equipment is taken out of service when it reaches the replacement age even if it still works.	Neutral
Warranties	No additional warranties are pursued beyond the standard warranty (1 year).	Extended warranties are purchased but don't cover the life of the equipment and doesn't include peripherals (3 year, computers only).	Extended warranties are purchased to extend the standard warranty on computers and peripherals but don't cover the equipment lifespan (3 year, all equipment).	Warranties are purchased to cover the life of the equipment (5 or more years).	$$$

www.iste.org — Developed by Dr. Chip Kimball (ckimball@iste.org) in conjunction with ISTE and the Gates Foundation.

Version 1.10

Technology Support Index

Page 3

Domain Two - Staffing and Processes

	Emergent	Islands	Integrated	Exemplary	Fiscal
Organizational Structure	Direction comes from multiple points within organization, and reporting isn't functionally logical. Cross-functional collaboration is difficult or non-existent.	The reporting structures are difficult to identify, and direction comes from multiple points of the organization. Cross-functional collaboration exists.	The technical support functions and instructional technology functions report through the same unit in the organization, but each unit is cohesively organized and there is communication between units.	All of the technology functions report through the same unit in the organization, providing for a logical chain of command and communication structures.	Neutral
Staffing to Computer Ratio	Computer-to-technician ratio is over 250:1.	Computer-to-technician ratio is between 150:1 and 250:1.	Computer-to-technician ratio is between 75:1 and 150:1.	Computer-to-technician ratio is less than 75:1.	$$$$
Formula-driven Technology Staffing (e.g., X computers + X network drops + X applications divided by Y = # of technicians)	Staffing formulas aren't used or considered.	Formulas for staffing are considered but are limited in scope and aren't used to drive staffing.	Comprehensive formulas have been developed, considering multiple dimensions of the environment, but are only used as a guide and don't drive staffing.	Comprehensive formulas have been developed and drive staffing as a normal part of operations. Formulas include multiple dimensions of the environment.	$$$$$
Escalation Process for Technical Issues	No escalation process is in place, and the path for resolution is unclear.	A clear path for resolution is in place, but no escalation process is recognized.	An escalation process is in place with two steps of escalation and significant crossover between levels.	A well-defined escalation process is in place, with three or more steps of escalation, and a clear path for resolution.	$
HelpDesk	No HelpDesk support is provided.	A help number is provided for staff but isn't fully staffed. The help number is used for emergencies, not as the first line of defense.	A district HelpDesk is in place, but district culture has not adopted the HelpDesk systemically.	A district HelpDesk is in place with trained staff, and the district culture embraces the HelpDesk as the first line of defense.	$$
Use of Online Knowledgebase for Technical Help	Staffs seek no help from online help both due to availability of resources and district culture.	Some staff seeks online help, but the behavior isn't pervasive.	Many staff seek online help, but not as their first line of defense.	Most staff seeks help from online knowledge bases as their first line of defense for most issues.	$$
Software Support Protocols and Standards	No list of supported software is provided for users.	A list of supported software is provided, but no differentiated processes are provided for limited support products.	A list of supported software is provided with differentiated processes; however, users and staff don't follow them closely.	A list of supported software is provided, with clear differentiated processes for each set of software that are consistently used.	Neutral
New Equipment Deployment	The school and local staff are responsible for the deployment of new equipment.	The technical staff manages deployment of new equipment requiring a reduction in regular service.	The manufacturer or a vendor does imaging and tagging of equipment, but setup is the responsibility of the regular technical staff.	The vendor deploys new equipment and includes imaging, asset tagging, setup, and network connections. Regular technical support functions aren't disrupted.	$$
Documented Procedures	Little or no documentation exists for technical tasks — requiring users and technical staff to invent their own solutions.	Some documentation exists for technical tasks but isn't widely shared or used. Most documentation is limited to few technical staff only.	Documentation exists for many technical tasks but is poorly written and isn't systematically updated as procedures are developed.	Documentation exists for most technical tasks and is used by most user groups. Well-written documentation production is a normal part of operations.	$$

iste

www.iste.org

Developed by Dr. Chip Kimball (ckimball@iste.org) in conjunction with ISTE and the Gates Foundation.

Version 1.10

Technology Support Index

Page 4

Domain Two - Staffing and Processes

	Emergent	Islands	Integrated	Exemplary	Fiscal
Certification of Technical Staff	Certification isn't a priority in the organization and concerns are raised about time away from the job to pursue certification.	Technical staff is encouraged to become certified, but no support is provided towards certification.	Some technical staff is certified in appropriate areas, others are involved in district-supported programs towards certification.	Most technical staff is certified in appropriate areas (e.g., A+, Cisco, MCSE, etc.).	$$
Differentiated Job Descriptions	Technical support employees do it all — and redundancies and inefficiencies are created as a result.	Technical support employees do it all, but redundancies aren't created due to size and/or staffing levels.	Some differentiation in jobs has occurred, although assignments aren't provided based upon skill-set competencies.	Job descriptions are fully differentiated creating specialization and efficiencies, and a clear avenue for support.	Neutral
Retention	Employee turnover is very high, and employee satisfaction is low.	Employee turnover is high due to other employment opportunities, and employee satisfaction is fair.	Employee turnover is moderate (excluding retirement), and employee satisfaction is high.	Employee turnover is very low (excluding retirement), and employee satisfaction is very high.	$
Competitive Compensation	Technical positions are poorly competitive, offering compensation in the bottom 50% of equivalent organizations in the area.	Technical positions are moderately competitive, offering compensation in the 50th to 75th percentile of equivalent organizations in the area.	Technical positions are competitive, offering compensation in the 75th to 90th percentile of equivalent organizations in the area, and offering competitive non-compensation benefits.	Technical positions are very competitive, offering compensation in the 90th percentile of equivalent organizations in the area, and in some cases, competing with private businesses for talent.	$$$
Certificated Support	Certificated employees provide all of the technical assistance in the building.	Certificated employees provide much of the technical assistance in the building with release time or stipend.	Certificated employees serve as the contact point, and perform some of the technical work in conjunction with technical staff.	Certificated employees are used as the contact point in the building, but don't perform technical support work.	Neutral
Contracted Support	Contracted support isn't used.	Contracted support is used rarely, typically for special projects only.	All technical support is contracted with an outside service organization and meets district criteria for support.	Contracted support is used for major projects and high-level technical problems, but not for day-to-day operational issues.	$$$
Student Support	Students provide support for the school in an ad-hoc manner due to limited district support.	Students are used extensively, in an official capacity and supplant district support.	No student support is provided.	A curricular program is designed to train students in technical support. They support district technology but in a peripheral way as part of their instructional program only.	Neutral

iste

Developed by Dr. Chip Kimball (ckimball@iste.org) in conjunction with ISTE and the Gates Foundation.

Technology Support Index

Domain Three - Professional Development

	Emergent	Islands	Integrated	Exemplary	Fiscal
Comprehensive Staff Development Programs	There is no formal staff development program in place, and training is provided infrequently. The organization depends upon individuals' own motivation to build expertise.	A staff development program is in place but is limited, voluntary, and uses a single dimension in its delivery.	A staff development program is in place. It isn't comprehensive in nature in that it doesn't impact all staff and doesn't offer the depth required to change the organization.	A comprehensive staff development program is in place that impacts ALL staff. The program is progressive in nature and balances incentive, accountability, and diverse learning opportunities.	$$$$
Online Training Opportunities	Online training opportunities don't exist.	Online training opportunities exist, but are limited in scope and are available to a limited population of employees.	Online training opportunities are available for staff onsite and remotely, but are limited in their offerings.	Online training opportunities are provided for staff both onsite and remotely, and represent a diversity of skill sets.	$$
Just-in-time Training	No just-in-time training process or delivery system has been put into place.	Just-in-time training is used, but the process and delivery system hasn't been refined so that it can be used realistically within the organization.	A process and delivery for just-in-time training is in place, but hasn't been adopted by the organization as a mechanism for solving issues.	A process and delivery system has been established for just-in-time training organization-wide and is used consistently.	$$
Expectations for All Staff	Expectations of staff aren't clearly defined and aren't part of the organizational culture.	Expectations of staff are articulated but are limited in scope.	Expectations of staff are articulated and are broad in scope, but have not been adopted as part of the organizational culture.	Expectations for all staff are clearly articulated and are broad in scope. Performance expectations are built into work functions and are part of the organizational culture.	Neutral
Training for Technical Staff	Technical staff is only given training to take care of the immediate issues in the district. Advanced training isn't encouraged.	Technical staff receives consistent training around emergent issues. Advanced training isn't district sponsored but is encouraged.	Technical staff receives consistent training around emergent issues and have limited district-sponsored opportunities for advanced training.	Technical staff receives ample training as a normal part of their employment, including training towards certification.	$$
Troubleshooting as Part of the Professional Development Program	Basic troubleshooting isn't considered part of professional development.	Troubleshooting is built into professional development, but is too technical in nature and isn't balanced with a technical support system.	Troubleshooting is built into the professional development program and is used as a major strategy for technical support.	Basic troubleshooting is built into the professional development program, and is used as a first line of defense in conjunction with technical support.	$

Developed by Dr. Chip Kimball (ckimball@iste.org) in conjunction with ISTE and the Gates Foundation.

Version 1.10

Technology Support Index

Domain Four - Intelligent Systems

	Emergent	Islands	Integrated	Exemplary	Fiscal
Trouble Ticketing System	No trouble ticketing system exists.	A simple trouble ticketing system is in place, but isn't electronic and/or is simple in its implementation, not allowing for universal tracking of issues and establishing trends.	A trouble ticketing system is in place and is used extensively for responding to technical issues. Analysis of issues, response times, and possible trends isn't done.	All technical issues are recorded and delegated to appropriate resources through an electronic trouble ticketing system. All technical issues are tracked and evaluated through this system.	$$
Virus Protection	No virus software is used.	Virus software is used, but it its client-based and therefore often out of date.	Server-based virus software is used, but the parameters for its use are loosely defined and updates aren't consistent.	Server-based virus software is available, used, and automatically updated.	$$
Network Infrastructure	Network access is limited and isn't available in every location.	Network access is available to all locations, but doesn't impact all computers and is limited in bandwidth.	Network access is available to all locations but segments of the network are limited in bandwidth.	Robust broadband network access is available to all locations allowing for unlimited network control and tool use.	$$$$
Desktop and Software Standardization Tools (Profiles)	No desktop standardization tools or practice are used.	Desktop standardization tools are in place, but are mostly ignored once the equipment is deployed.	Desktop standardization tools are in place, but changes users make aren't automatically corrected.	Desktop standardization tools are used to provide a common desktop for all users and access to common software. Changes to the desktop are automatically corrected.	$
Network Sniffing Tools	No network sniffing tools are used.	Network sniffing tools are used for problem diagnosis only.	Network sniffing tools are used for problem diagnosis and limited preventative maintenance.	Network sniffing tools are used to both diagnose problems and establish performance matrices for preventative maintenance. The network is systematically monitored using these tools.	$$
Online Knowledgebase	No online knowledgebase is present.	An online knowledgebase is in place, but it is limited in scope and isn't readily used in the organization.	An online knowledgebase is in place and is employed by users. It isn't designed to easily expand and users don't use it as a first line of defense.	An online knowledgebase is in place and is expansive in its detail. It is used readily and automatically grows based upon trend data generated in other tracking systems.	$$
Integrated and Systemic Electronic Communication	Electronic communication is limited and has little use for providing technical support.	Electronic communication is available to many staff but isn't integrated at all into the daily work of employees.	Electronic communication is available to everyone in the organization but isn't readily used for technical support.	Electronic communication is available to everyone in the organization and is integrated into daily work so that it can be used for technical support.	$
Remote Computer Management	No remote management is available.	Remote management is available for servers only.	Remote management is available for all computers but isn't used extensively.	Remote management is available for all computers and is used as a primary strategy of support.	$$$

iste

Developed by Dr. Chip Kimball (ckimball@iste.org) in conjunction with ISTE and the Gates Foundation.

Version 1.10

Technology Support Index

Domain Four - Intelligent Systems

	Emergent	Islands	Integrated	Exemplary	Fiscal
Ghost or other imaging systems	Ghost or imaging systems aren't used.	Imaging software is used in the most primitive sense — only providing recovery services with the imaging software provided by the vendor.	An image is used for delivery of the machine but isn't used to clone all of the software on the machine. Only the basic OS and basic software is imaged. Imaging is used as a troubleshooting strategy.	Imaging software is used for delivery of new machines, and as a troubleshooting strategy. Software installed through the imaging process is comprehensive.	$
Systems Management Server (SMS) or ManageWise	SMS or ManageWise isn't used as a district tool.	SMS or ManageWise is used for metering but isn't used for installation and updates, and its use is limited in scope.	SMS or ManageWise is used for metering and some software updates, but major software installations are handled on the individual PC.	SMS or ManageWise is used for all software distribution, technical updates, and for metering of software use on the district's computers.	$$
Server Farms and Centralized Services	Every site has its own server and, in some cases, multiple servers. Backup and server management takes place locally.	Each site has only one server with some services (e.g., e-mail, student information system [SIS]) provided centrally.	Many servers are consolidated into a few locations and most services are provided centrally.	All servers and services are centralized requiring minimal server management outside of one location.	$$$
Use of Application Service Providers (ASP)	No ASP services are utilized.	One or two ASP services are used, but it doesn't impact support due to the peripheral nature of the product.	A number of ASP services are used but is limited to one category of software (e.g., productivity, research, libraries, content, etc.).	ASP services are used for most major applications, including productivity, content, and research based applications.	$$$
Thin-client Computing	Thin-client computing isn't used.	Thin-client is used but is limited to a small number of users for specific applications.	Thin-client is used for most users of administrative systems and some productivity software.	All administrative and productivity software for staff is delivered through a thin-client model.	$$$
Vendor-specific Management Tools (e.g., Insight Manager)	Vendor tools aren't installed or considered when purchasing hardware.	Vendor tools are available and have been purchased but are mostly unused.	Vendor tools are used in a limited way for diagnosis and prevention.	Vendor tools are used extensively for diagnosis of issues, to streamline processes, and for preventive measures.	$
Quality Assurance (QA) and Customer Follow-up	Surveys are conducted generally as part of other departmental survey work within the organization or not at all.	QA surveys are conducted, but they aren't automated and are only done annually.	Surveys specific to technical support are conducted. However, they are done only periodically, and the data is used sporadically.	QA is measured by a random and automatic system that tracks customer satisfaction and closed tickets. Data is collected throughout the year. Questions asked are specific to technical support and the data is used to make adjustments.	$
Student/Fiscal/HR/ Assessment Systems	Student/Fiscal/HR/Assessment systems aren't in place.	Student/Fiscal/HR/Assessment systems are partially in place, and aren't reliable or intuitive.	Student/Fiscal/HR/Assessment systems are in place and are reliable, but don't integrate well with other systems and aren't intuitive.	Student/Fiscal/HR/Assessment systems are in place, reliable, intuitive, and integrate nicely with other productivity tools.	$$$

www.iste.org

Developed by Dr. Chip Kimball (ckimball@iste.org) in conjunction with ISTE and the Gates Foundation.

Appendix

About the Authors

An editor and writer, Paige Leavitt has helped to produce and publish a number of APQC publications, including the Passport to Success series and Best-practice Reports. She is the author of *Solving Problems in Schools: A Guide for Educators* (2003) and co-author of *Capturing Critical Knowledge From a Shifting Work Force* (2003), *Content Management* Passport Guide (2003), *Competitive Intelligence* Passport Guide (2004), and *The Executive's Role in Knowledge Management* (2004). Before joining APQC, Leavitt edited language arts textbooks for Holt, Rinehart & Winston.

Randy McDaniel received his doctorate in educational leadership from Wichita State University and has served in public education for the past 20 years as a classroom teacher, building administrator, and in central office leadership roles. McDaniel has presented nationally on such topics as curriculum, strategic planning, Web-based education, instructional technology, and educational leadership.

Additionally, he serves as school accreditation on-site chair for several Kansas school districts and on many advisory boards and committees for various educational organizations. A former superintendent of Iola, Kansas USD 257 and a former professor of educational leadership at Pittsburg State University, McDaniel is currently president and CEO of VRSchoolhouse. VRSchoolhouse provides online courses, curriculum and instructional management systems, and consulting services to schools across the nation.

Emma Skogstad is a freelance writer and editor in Austin, Texas, and co-owner of SYA Editorial Consultants, an educational development house specializing in state-specific standardized test preparation for middle school and high school. Skogstad has worked as an in-house editor in the language arts departments at Glencoe/McGraw-Hill and Holt, Rinehart & Winston. She has written several articles for APQC and edited *Solving Problems in Schools: A Guide for Educators* (2003).

Appendix

About the American Productivity & Quality Center

An internationally recognized resource for process and performance improvement, the American Productivity & Quality Center (APQC) helps organizations adapt to rapidly changing environments, build new and better ways to work, and succeed in a competitive marketplace. With a focus on benchmarking, knowledge management, metrics, performance measurement, and quality improvement initiatives, APQC works with its member organizations to identify best practices, discover effective methods of improvement, broadly disseminate findings, and connect individuals with one another and the knowledge, training, and tools they need to succeed. Founded in 1977, APQC is a member-based nonprofit serving organizations around the world in all sectors of business, education, and government.

Today, APQC works with organizations across all industries to find practical, cost-effective solutions to drive productivity and quality improvement. APQC offers a variety of products and services including:

- consortium, custom, and metric benchmarking studies;
- publications, including books, Best-practice Reports, and implementation guides;
- computer-based, on-site, and custom training;
- consulting and facilitation services; and
- networking opportunities.

PUBLICATIONS

APQC is the preeminent source for leading-edge organizational research and improvement information. Designed to ease your way to positive results, APQC publications come in many forms and cover a wide range of subjects. APQC has a number of publications created specifically for educators that are focused on using data-driven instructional tools and strategies to improve student and system performance. Popular titles from APQC's quickly expanding publications catalog include:

- *8 Steps to Student Success* by Mary Barksdale and Patricia Davenport
- *A Guide to Reinventing Schools* by the Re-Inventing Schools Coalition
- *Benchmarking Best Practices in Accountability Systems in Education*
- *Benchmarking in Education: Pure & Simple*
- *Closing the Achievement Gap: No Excuses* by Gerald Anderson and Patricia Davenport
- *Continuous Improvement Tools in Education: Volume 1*
- *Continuous Improvement Tools in Education: Volume 2*
- *Educators in Action: Examining Successful Improvement Efforts* (to be released fall 2004)
- *Improving Teacher Education and Preparation*
- *PDCA Instructional Cycle*
- *Solving Problems in Schools: A Guide for Educators* by Paige Leavitt
- *Today's Teaching and Learning: Leveraging Technology*

These and other titles can be ordered through APQC's online bookstore at www.apqc.org/pubs.